THRIVING BOARDS WORKBOOK
Growing Healthy, Effective Camp Boards

An Initiative of
Christian Camp and Conference Association
4th Edition

THRIVING BOARDS WORKBOOK ◆ Growing Healthy, Effective Camp Boards
4th Edition – CCCA Thriving Boards Leadership and Development Program
An Initiative of Christian Camp and Conference Association
https://www.ccca.org/ccca/Thriving_Boards.asp

For more information:
Gregg Hunter
President/CEO
Christian Camp and Conference Association
P.O. Box 62189
Colorado Springs, CO 80962-2189
Phone: (719) 260-9400
Fax: (719) 260-6398
www.ccca.org

© **September 2019, Christian Camp and Conference Association**

All rights reserved. No part of this publication may be reproduced in any form without written permission from Christian Camp and Conference Association. Permission is given to cohort participants (and purchasers of this workbook) to use these materials within your own organization.

Many of the book reviews and links to book reviews are from *Your Weekly Staff Meeting eNewsletter*, published and edited by John Pearson and used by permission. Reviews of many of the books mentioned can be located online by searching "[book title], *John Pearson's Buckets Blog.*" Archives of the reviews are posted at https://urgentink.typepad.com/my_weblog/.

While the intellectual property in this volume is owned by Christian Camp and Conference Association, some of the materials herein have been copyrighted, separately, by the author and/or presenter, and/or previous presenters in the Thriving Boards Program.

Ed McDowell
Thriving Boards Lead Facilitator and Workbook Editor
www.standpoint360.com

ORDER ADDITIONAL COPIES: www.Amazon.com

Printed in the USA by: Amazon Kindle Direct Publishing
ISBN: (see back cover)

FALL SESSION

	TITLE	PAGE
	Introduction: 6 Ways to Invest in Your Board	5
	Thriving Boards Bonus Resources: Leaders Are Readers!	7
	Healthy Governance Checklist	10
1	Balancing Board Roles – The 3 Hats: Governance, Volunteer, Participant	13
2	Improving and Enriching the Board Experience by Focusing on Board Recruitment	33
3	Breakout With Your Coach	47
4	Leading From a Healthy Governance Model: Creating Clarity and Alignment	55
5	Leveraging the 3 Powerful S's: Spiritual Gifts, Social Styles, Strengths	69
6	Keeping the Promise: A Special Presentation	89
7	A Board Prayer	91
8	The Board's Role in Embracing the Donor (Part 1)	95
9	Strategic Planning: Does Your Board Own the Strategy?	107
10	Succession Planning: The Board Should Do What Only the Board Can Do	119
11	Strategic Next Steps and My One Big Take-Away	125

SPRING SESSION

	TITLE	PAGE
12	Reporting In: Organizational Progress Reports	135
13	The Board's Financial/Fiduciary Roles: The BPM Practicum	139
14	The Board's Financial/Fiduciary Role: Long-Term Sustainability	149
15	Strategic Tools and Templates for Board Best Practices and Sustainability	169
16	The Evening Dessert Hour: Continuing the Promise	175
17	Board Service: A Sacred Trust	177
18	The Board's Role in Owning the Assumptions… …That Undergird Our Business Model and Strategic Plan	181
19	The Board's Role in Embracing the Donor (Part 2)	195
20	Coach Time: Our Strategic Next Steps and Healthy Governance Checklist	207
21	Strategic Next Steps and My One Big Take-Away	211
	Appendix: Recommended Books and Resources	217

A greeter at Walmart gets more orientation than most board members ever do.[1]

Patrick Lencioni

---

[1] Quoted in *Lessons From the Nonprofit Boardroom: 40 Insights for Better Board Meetings, Second Edition*, by Dan Busby and John Pearson (Winchester, VA: ECFAPress, 2018), 202.

INTRODUCTION: 6 Ways to Invest in Your Board

Whether you're a participant in the CCCA Thriving Boards Leadership and Development Program...or you're reading through this workbook with your board—you are about to embark on a ministry-changing experience! Thank you for investing in The Power of Camp!

Ed McDowell
Lead Facilitator
CCCA Thriving Boards Leadership and Development Program

Here are six ways to get the most out of this program—and this workbook!

❑ **1. Leverage today as the first day of your lifelong governance journey.** If God has called you to serve on your camp's board—He has called you to effective preparation, prayer, and diligence. We're grateful that airline pilots and surgeons are lifelong learners—and campers, parents, families, and churches will also be grateful that your camp's board members are also lifelong learners!

❑ **2. Identify your "1 BIG Take-Away" for each session—and share it with your colleagues (or tweet it!).** As you participate in the program (or read this workbook on your own), pause at the completion of each session/chapter—and identify your "1 BIG Take-Away." Share that important learning with a colleague—or tweet it!

❑ **3. With your colleagues, identify your "Top-5 Strategic Next Steps."** After completing this program—or reading this workbook—don't stress out! It may take you two or three years to implement some of the ideas and concepts from the CCCA Thriving Boards Program. Pray, discern, and trust God for next steps. Then...start with your "Top-5 Strategic Next Steps." *But don't be frightened by the size of the task!*

Take this cue from King David in his charge to Solomon in 1 Chronicles 28:19-21 (TLB):

> "Every part of this blueprint," David told Solomon, "was given to me in writing from the hand of the Lord." Then he continued, "Be strong and courageous and get to work. **Don't be frightened by the size of the task, for the Lord my God is with you; he will not forsake you.** He will see to it that everything is finished correctly. And these various groups of priests and Levites will serve in the Temple. Others with skills of every kind will volunteer, and the army and the entire nation are at your command."

❑ **4. Give a copy of this workbook to every board member—and share highlights of the Thriving Boards sessions at your next board meeting.** Ask board members to give brief reports of their BIG take-aways at future board meetings. Ask the full board for input on your "Top-5 Strategic Next Steps" and (perhaps with board action, recorded in the minutes) affirm your next steps. Then—add "next steps" to your agenda and bring a progress report at every board meeting. (*And—be sure there is progress!*)

If you did not attend the Thriving Boards Program:
❑ **5. Become a lifelong learner!** Select one or two governance resources recommended in this workbook—and invest time in enhancing your competences in God-honoring governance.

Review the resources and books that were included in the program—and volunteer to read and report on one of those books at a future board meeting. Reminder:

Leadership is a complex field and no one resource can meet all the needs of every leader in every situation.[2]

Richard Kriegbaum

❏ **6. Appoint a "Leaders Are Readers Champion!"** Read Lesson 38, "Great Boards Delegate Their Reading," in *Lessons From the Nonprofit Boardroom,* and inspire your board to invest "10 Minutes for Governance" in every board meeting (see Lesson 39).

Greetings from Gregg Hunter

Your service as a camp/conference board member inspires us! It's our prayer that the CCCA Thriving Boards Leadership and Development Program will energize a holy ripple effect across our nation—and globally! Thank you for investing your valuable time as a board member and steward of God's work in your important ministry. *It has eternal consequences.*

Gregg Hunter
President/CEO
Christian Camp and Conference Association

Special Thanks to Murdock Trust!

CCCA gratefully acknowledges the vision and generosity of the M.J. Murdock Charitable Trust for their extraordinary partnership in the partial funding of the CCCA Thriving Boards Leadership and Development Program. The Trust's mission is "to serve individuals, families and communities across the Pacific Northwest by providing grants and enrichment programs to organizations that strengthen the region's educational, social, spiritual and cultural base in creative and sustainable ways."

We are especially appreciative of the vision for this program by Terry Stokesbary, Senior Program Director for Enrichment Initiatives, and the support and encouragement of Steve Moore, Executive Director.

For more information, visit: www.murdocktrust.org.

"Now it is required that those who have been given a trust must prove faithful." 1 Corinthians 4:2 (*NIV*)	"Put God in charge of your work Then what you've planned will take place." Proverbs 16:3 (*The Message*)

---

[2] Quoted in *Lessons From the Nonprofit Boardroom,* by Dan Busby and John Pearson, 202.

THRIVING BOARDS BONUS RESOURCES:
Leaders Are Readers!

Each camp and conference center that participates in the CCCA Thriving Boards Leadership and Development Program will receive the following resources. Boards are urged to "delegate your reading" to other board members and spread the joy of lifelong learning!

FALL SESSION:

Ten Basic Responsibilities of Nonprofit Boards
Richard T. Ingram

Owning Up: The 14 Questions Every Board Member Needs to Ask
Ram Charan

Scaling Up: How a Few Companies Make It...and Why the Rest Don't – Mastering the Rockefeller Habits 2.0
Verne Harnish

ECFA 3rd Annual Nonprofit Governance Survey
ECFA Press

StrengthsFinder 2.0: Discover Your CliftonStrengths
From Gallup and Tom Rath

Peter Drucker's Five Most Important Questions: Enduring Wisdom for Today's Leaders
Peter F. Drucker, Frances Hesselbein, and Joan Snyder Kuhl

Nonprofit Sustainability: Making Strategic Decisions for Financial Viability
Jeanne Bell, Jan Masaoka and Steve Zimmerman

ECFA Tools and Templates for Effective Board Governance: Time-Saving Solutions for Your Board
Dan Busby and John Pearson

SPRING SESSION:

Development 101: Building a Comprehensive Development Program on Biblical Values
John R. Frank
and R. Scott Rodin

The ONE Thing: The Surprisingly Simple Truth Behind Extraordinary Results
Gary Keller
with Jay Papasan

Call of the Chair: Leading the Board of the Christ-centered Ministry
David L. McKenna

*Lessons From the Nonprofit Boardroom:
40 Insights for Better Board Meetings (Second Edition)*
Dan Busby and John Pearson

40 Guest Bloggers! Read color commentaries on all 40 lessons from Gregg Hunter, Ed McDowell, Bob King, Mike Pate, Dan Bolin and others at:

http://nonprofitboardroom.blogspot.com/

ECFA GOVERNANCE TOOLBOX SERIES: www.ECFA.org/toolbox

Note! Thriving Boards participants will receive online access to these four toolboxes from ECFA.
- ✓ Step 1: Create an account at www.ECFA.org/toolbox
- ✓ Step 2: Order the toolbox of your choice.
- ✓ Step 3: Enter the promo code provided by Thriving Boards: _____

ECFA GOVERNANCE TOOLBOX
Series No. 1 - Recruiting Board Members
Leveraging the 4 Phases of Board Recruitment:
Cultivation, Recruitment, Orientation and Engagement

ECFA GOVERNANCE TOOLBOX
Series No. 2 - Balancing Board Roles
Understanding the 3 Board Hats: Governance, Volunteer, Participant

ECFA GOVERNANCE TOOLBOX
Series No. 3 - Conflicts of Interest
Addressing Board and Organizational Conflicts of Interest

ECFA GOVERNANCE TOOLBOX
Series No. 4 - Succession Planning
Eleven Principles for Successful Successions

Each toolbox includes:
- ☑ Online video (10-12 minutes)
- ☑ *Board Member Read-and-Engage Viewing Guide*
- ☑ *Facilitator Guide*
- ☑ Access to hidden webpage resources

HEALTHY GOVERNANCE CHECKLIST:
Moving to Board Health in 24 to 36 months!

➔**NOTE:** The book, *Scaling Up* by Verne Harnish, leverages the *Rockefeller Habits Checklist™*, 40 critical "habits" that the team must address in 10 major areas.

You can download a one-page copy of the *Rockefeller Habits Checklist™* at the author's company website (including other tools) here: www.ScalingUp.com. You can also download it here: https://gazelles.com/static/resources/tools/en/RH_Checklist.pdf

Using the concept of the *Rockefeller Habits Checklist™*, the following pages feature "Version 1.0" of the *Thriving Boards Healthy Governance Checklist*. Your input and feedback is invited!

Verne Harnish

"**WARNING: You'll drive everyone in the organization crazy if you implement all of these habits at one time.** The key is focusing on one or two each quarter, giving everyone roughly 24 to 36 months to install these simple, yet powerful routines. Then it's a process of continually refreshing them as the company scales up." (See page 15 and read why habits are "routines that set you free!")[3]

☑ HEALTHY GOVERNANCE CHECKLIST (by session number)
CCCA Thriving Boards ◆ Growing Healthy, Effective Boards

#1. EVERY BOARD MEMBER UNDERSTANDS THE THREE BOARD HATS.
- ❏ The GOVERNANCE hat is policy-oriented and worn only during board meetings (and never when volunteering).
- ❏ The VOLUNTEER hat is optional and is not worn during board meetings.
- ❏ The PARTICIPANT hat is worn at "required attendance" events for board members (identified a year in advance).
- ❏ *The Board Member Annual Affirmation Statement* details the roles and responsibilities of board members (based on the three hats) and this document is signed and affirmed by all board members every January.

#2. NEW BOARD MEMBERS ARE RECRUITED *SLOWLY*...WITH DISCERNMENT.
- ❏ CULTIVATION: We have written board member criteria and pray before prospecting.
- ❏ RECRUITMENT: We "date" prospects before proposing marriage and guide them into the circles of involvement.
- ❏ ORIENTATION: We have a written new board member orientation process that spans about six months.
- ❏ ENGAGEMENT: We have high expectations (in writing) of all board members and leverage their "3 Powerful S's."

#4. THE BOARD AFFIRMS ITS GOVERNANCE MODEL AND THEOLOGY.
- ❏ All board members acknowledge their sacred trust as "stewards," not "owners" of the ministry.
- ❏ Board members have a basic understanding of John Carver's "Policy Governance®" model and the four key areas: 1) ends (the taxi), 2) executive limitations (the corral), 3) board-staff linkage, and 4) governing process.
- ❏ Board members agree on where the board is—currently—on the continuum between "policy-making governance" and "hands-on governance"—and where the board wants to be within 12 to 18 months.
- ❏ Board members agree on where their CEO is—currently—on the leadership continuum between "proactive leadership" and "reactive leadership"—and where the board wants the CEO to be within 12 to 18 months.

---

[3] Verne Harnish, *Scaling Up: How a Few Companies Make It...and Why the Rest Don't—Mastering the Rockefeller Habits 2.0* (USA: Gazelles, 2014), 15.

☑ HEALTHY GOVERNANCE CHECKLIST (by session number)
CCCA Thriving Boards ◆ Growing Healthy, Effective Boards

#5. ALL BOARD MEMBERS LEVERAGE THEIR "SWEET SPOTS" WHEN SERVING!
- ☐ Board members understand board service as a holy calling—and experience joy when serving.
- ☐ The board leverages the spiritual gifts, social styles (or other model), and strengths of each other.
- ☐ Board members are students of the unique strengths and giftedness of their board chair and their CEO.
- ☐ The board chair, CEO and the senior team are students of the strengths and giftedness of all board members.

#7. THE BOARD PRIORITIZES PRAYER AND DISCERNMENT IN EVERY BOARD MEETING.
- ☐ We are clear that we are stewards, not owners, of the ministry—and we prepare agendas with prayer.
- ☐ While we often pray at the beginning and the end of our meetings, we also interject prayers of adoration, confession, thanksgiving, and supplication—throughout our meetings.
- ☐ We are increasingly moving from mere "decision-making" to discernment—as the Holy Spirit guides us.[4]
- ☐ We pray for the "joy of arriving at adjournment closer to one another because we are closer" to our Lord.

#8. BOARD MEMBERS AFFIRM THEIR IMPORTANT ROLES WITH DONORS.
- ☐ Board member recruitment and orientation includes expectations about generous giving.
- ☐ Board member recruitment and orientation includes affirmations about building relationships with others.
- ☐ Board members are coached and each board member's development role is customized according to a board member's 3 Powerful S's (Spiritual Gifts, Strengths, and Social Styles—see Session 5).
- ☐ Board members affirm and live out the ministry's written "Theology of Development."[5]

#9. THE BOARD AFFIRMS THE STRATEGIC PLAN AND OWNS THE STRATEGY.
- ☐ The board ensures that a robust strategic planning process is built into the organization's DNA—year-round.
- ☐ The staff creates the strategic plan—with significant counsel from the board—and the board approves the plan.
- ☐ The strategic plan is forward-looking and visionary, and is graphically visualized with tools such as "The Rolling 3-Year Strategic Plan" (a one-page summary) and a Big HOLY Audacious Goal (BHAG).
- ☐ A two-page strategy document is available at every board meeting—and the board OWNS the strategy.

#10. THE BOARD HAS WRITTEN CONTINGENCY PLANS AND SUCCESSION PLANS IN THE EVENT OF A LEADERSHIP TRANSITION (PLANNED OR UNPLANNED).
- ☐ The full board reviews the written Contingency Plan and written Succession Plan at least annually.
- ☐ The board chair and the CEO regularly affirm that any "elephants in the room" (concerning succession) are appropriately addressed in a timely manner.
- ☐ The full board conducts a CEO performance review at least annually and the CEO recommends a written professional development plan in response to the performance review.
- ☐ The CEO is responsible annually for formally updating the Board on the training, development and leadership potential of all of his/her direct reports, including any high capacity people further down in the organization.

---

[4] Ruth Haley Barton, *Pursuing God's Will Together: A Discernment Practice for Leadership Groups* (Downers Grove, IL: InterVarsity Press, 2012).

[5] John R. Frank and R. Scott Rodin, *Development 101: Building a Comprehensive Development Program on Biblical Values* (Colbert, WA: Kingdom Life Publishing and Steward Publishing, 2015) 7-17. (See also "An Example of a Theology of Development" on pages 143-148.)

☑ HEALTHY GOVERNANCE CHECKLIST (by session number)
CCCA Thriving Boards ◆ Growing Healthy, Effective Boards

#13. BOARD MEMBERS ARE DILIGENT IN THEIR FIDUCIARY GOVERNANCE ROLES.
- ❑ The board's governance documents clearly articulate the financial, legal, and fiduciary roles of board members.
- ❑ Board members trust God as they steward their fiduciary governance roles and responsibilities, especially related to the bylaws; local, state, and federal laws and regulations; financial audits and program audits; financial controls and cash reserves; CEO compensation-setting policies; accreditation; and other written responsibilities.
- ❑ The board regularly updates the *Board Policies Manual (BPM)* or a similar policy document.
- ❑ The board ensures that the CEO and financial team are focused on "The 7 Key Financial Levers."[6]

#14. THE BOARD MONITORS BOTH FINANCIAL AND PROGRAMMATIC HEALTH.
- ❑ The board regularly reviews key indicators of financial health—and the importance and status of cash.
- ❑ The board regularly reviews key indicators that measure the health of the organization's programs, products, and services.
- ❑ The board affirms the organization's Business Model Statement.
- ❑ The board appropriately balances mission impact and sustainability—and discerns the organization's budget, and program priorities in light of Kingdom impact.

#15. THE BOARD APPROVES A SHORT LIST OF TOOLS AND TEMPLATES THAT WILL ENHANCE TRUST, INFORMATION FLOW, AND EFFECTIVE GOVERNANCE.
- ❑ The board affirms the standard format of agendas, written reports, recommendations, and minutes for all board meetings (including before, during, and after board meetings).
- ❑ The board affirms the standard format and frequency of CEO written reports—between board meetings.
- ❑ The board affirms the frequency and deadlines of all reports (example: seven days before a board meeting…).
- ❑ At least annually, the CEO and board chair review the effectiveness of the current tools and templates and, if needed, recommend changes to the board.

#18. THE BOARD OWNS THE ASSUMPTIONS THAT UNDERGIRD THE BUSINESS MODEL AND THE STRATEGIC PLAN.
- ❑ Board members engage in a staff/board/stakeholder planning process that includes the consideration of numerous assumptions—culminating in a thoughtful list of "Our Top-10 Assumptions for 20___."
- ❑ The board affirms the annual written document, "Our Top-10 Assumptions for 20___."
- ❑ Every board member engages regularly with key volunteers, donors, primary customers, supporting customers, and others to solicit feedback on "Our Top-10 Assumptions for 20___."
- ❑ Board members ensure that there is alignment between the Top-10 Assumptions and the business model and strategic plan—and prayer and discernment undergirds this year-round feedback process.

---

[6] See page 231 in *Scaling Up*, by Verne Harnish, and read "The Power of One and the 7 Levers" which include: 1) Price, 2) Volume, 3) Costs of goods sold/direct costs, 4) Operating expenses, 5) Accounts receivable, 6) Inventory/work in progress, and 7) Accounts payable.

SESSION 1

Balancing Board Roles

The 3 Hats:
- ☑ Governance
- ☑ Volunteer
- ☑ Participant

SESSION 1:
Balancing Board Roles: The 3 Hats
Governance, Volunteer, Participant

> ☑ **HEALTHY GOVERNANCE CHECKLIST**
> **CCCA Thriving Boards ◆ Growing Healthy, Effective Boards**
>
> **#1. EVERY BOARD MEMBER UNDERSTANDS THE THREE BOARD HATS.**
> ❏ The GOVERNANCE hat is policy-oriented and worn only during board meetings (and never when volunteering).
> ❏ The VOLUNTEER hat is optional and is not worn during board meetings.
> ❏ The PARTICIPANT hat is worn at "required attendance" events for board members (identified a year in advance).
> ❏ *The Board Member Annual Affirmation Statement* details the roles and responsibilities of board members (based on the three hats) and this document is signed and affirmed by all board members every January.

IN THIS SESSION:

❏ 1. <u>Two Books</u>: Clarify the Confusion Between Board Roles and Staff Roles
  ✓ *Ten Basic Responsibilities of Nonprofit Boards*
  ✓ *Ten Basic Responsibilities of CEOs*

❏ 2. <u>Video</u>: Balancing Board Roles: The Board Member's 3 Hats

❏ 3. <u>Tool</u>: The Board Member Annual Affirmation Statement

❏ 4. <u>Best Practice When Wearing the Governance Hat</u>: Annually Affirm the "CEO Annual S.M.A.R.T. Goals and Monthly Dashboard Report"

Session 1 ◆ Balancing Board Roles

❏ 1. TWO BOOKS: Clarify the Confusion Between Board Roles and Staff Roles
- ✓ *Ten Basic Responsibilities of Nonprofit Boards*
- ✓ *Ten Basic Responsibilities of CEOs*

First…define reality:

	☑ POP QUIZ!	YES	NO	NOT SURE
1	The roles and responsibilities for our CEO are in written form.			
2	The roles and responsibilities for our CEO have been reviewed and affirmed by the board (or Executive Committee) in the last 24 months.			
3	The roles and responsibilities for our CEO align with our tentative direction on these two continuums: ❏ BOARD: High Policy-making (10)……High Hands-on (1) ❏ CEO: Proactive Leader (10)…………..Reactive Leader (1)			
4	The board has reviewed and approved 3 to 5 "CEO Annual **S.M.A.R.T.** Goals" for this year—and they are in written form in board minutes. • **S**pecific • **M**easurable • **A**chievable • **R**ealistic • **T**ime-Related			
5	Our CEO provides a one-page monthly or quarterly dashboard report to the board, noting the status/progress on his/her 3 to 5 "CEO Annual S.M.A.R.T. Goals" for this year.			
6	Yikes! None of the above!			

"There are three roles of the CEO:
selecting the right people,
allocating capital resources,
and spreading ideas quickly."[7]

---

[7] Jack Welch, quoted in "Leadership Tip of the Day" email from the (now named) "Francis Hesselbein Leadership Forum," June 4, 2015, www.HesselbeinForum.org.

Ten Basic Responsibilities of Nonprofit Boards
Third Edition
by Richard Ingram

Ten Basic Responsibilities of Nonprofit Boards[8]	☑ Check…if this is included in your board's current position description. ☒ Note…any action steps required.
1 Determine mission and purpose, and advocate for them	
2 Select the chief executive	
3 Support and evaluate the chief executive	
4 Ensure effective planning	
5 Monitor and strengthen programs and services	
6 Ensure adequate financial resources	
7 Protect assets and provide financial oversight	
8 Build a competent board	
9 Ensure legal and ethical integrity	
10 Enhance the organization's public standing	

HOMEWORK! We would add these additional board responsibilities—based on our history, our culture, our faith-based convictions, the season/cycle we're in, and other factors:

11	
12	
13	
14	
15	

➔ _____ has volunteered to read this book and share a brief book review at a future board meeting.

---

[8] Richard T. Ingram, *Ten Basic Responsibilities of Nonprofit Boards, Third Edition*, (Washington, DC: BoardSource, 2015), v-vi.

The Nonprofit Chief Executive's Ten Basic Responsibilities
Second Edition
by Rick Moyers

CHAPTER TITLES:

	10 Basic Responsibilities of Nonprofit CEOs	☑ Check…if this is included in your current CEO position description. ☒ Note…any action steps required.
1	Commit to the Mission	
2	Lead the Staff and Manage the Organization	
3	Exercise Responsible Financial Stewardship	
4	Lead and Manage Fundraising	
5	Follow the Highest Ethical Standards, Ensure Accountability, and Comply with the Law	
6	Engage the Board in Planning and Lead Implementation	
7	Develop Future Leadership	
8	Build External Relationships and Serve as an Advocate	
9	Ensure the Quality and Effectiveness of Programs	
10	Support the Board	

HOMEWORK! We would add these additional basic responsibilities—based on our history, our culture, our faith-based convictions, the season/cycle we're in, and other factors:

11	
12	
13	
14	
15	

➔**NOTE:** The book includes "Ten Questions for Nonprofit CEOs" on pages 59-62, including:

#6. Do you know who your next board chair is likely to be?
❑ Yes   ❑ No   ❑ Are you kidding?

Session 1 ◆ Balancing Board Roles

#2. VIDEO: Balancing Board Roles - The Board Member's 3 Hats

www.ecfa.org/toolbox
→ Contact CCCA Thriving Boards for promo code: [　　　　　　　　]

❑ **ECFA Governance Toolbox Series No. 2:**
Balancing Board Roles: Understanding the 3 Board Hats
  ❑ Governance
  ❑ Volunteer
  ❑ Participant

Each Toolbox includes:
  ❑ Online video
  ❑ *Board Member Read-and-Engage Viewing Guide*
  ❑ *Facilitator Guide*
  ❑ Access to tools, templates, and resources on hidden webpage

DOWNLOAD: *Board Member Annual Affirmation Statement* (sample template - identifying the "3 Hats of a Board Member") – see the following pages.

→ **Note!** This resource will also provide access to the *Board Member Annual Affirmation Statement* (Word document) so you can customize it for your board's unique use.

ECFA Tools and Templates for Effective Board Governance: Time-Saving Solutions for Your Board, by Dan Busby and John Pearson[9]

---

[9] Dan Busby and John Pearson, *ECFA Tools and Templates for Effective Board Governance: Time-Saving Solutions for Your Board* (Winchester, VA: ECFAPress, 2019)

Session 1 ♦ Balancing Board Roles

VIDEO NOTES: The Board Member's 3 Hats

WORKSHEET:

THE STORY	
THE 3 HATS	❑ The Governance Hat ❑ The Volunteer Hat ❑ The Participant Hat
THE PRINCIPLE	If you need a board member, _____. If you need a volunteer, _____.

Session 1 ◆ Balancing Board Roles

WORKSHEET: What hat are you wearing when…
☑ Check one box per row.

BOARD MEMBER HATS	GOVERNANCE HAT	VOLUNTEER HAT	PARTICIPANT HAT
#1. "It's important that we have several board members present when our Rescue Mission Graduates receive their diplomas next week."			
#2. "All in favor say 'aye.'"			
#3. "As you know, every board member and spouse must host a table at our annual fundraising dinner—and invite eight guests."			
#4. "The staff needs some accounting help to close the year-end books."			
#5. "The Audit and Finance Committee will meet with the auditor on July 15."			
#6. "Frankly, my staff can't understand why more board members don't show up at our workdays and walk-a-thons. They don't think you support the ministry—nor have any idea what's going on."			
#7. "Fred, it sounds like you have passion in that area. As chairman, I'm asking you to chair a task force to pick the colors and carpeting for our new office remodel."			
#8. "Due to our CEO's accident, he needs help on Draft #2 of the strategic plan. Any takers?"			
#9. "Our day of prayer is next Thursday. All board members are expected to come. We'll also have a quick business meeting before the prayer services begin."			
#10.			

Session 1 ◆ Balancing Board Roles

SAMPLE ONLY - not prescriptive for your organization

Board Member Annual Affirmation Statement

A resource to supplement the materials in the **ECFA Governance Toolbox Series No. 2: Balancing Board Roles** Understanding the 3 Board Hats: Governance ▶ Volunteer ▶ Participant ▶ www.ecfa.org/toolbox

"With crystal clarity, we explain the 3 distinct hats of board service: Governance, Volunteer and Participant."
ECFA Governance Toolbox Series No. 1: Recruiting Board Members
Board Member Read-and-Engage Viewing Guide (page 11)

How to use this document:
Begin by asking your board members to answer three questions:

HOW STRONGLY DO YOU AGREE OR DISAGREE WITH THESE STATEMENTS?
1 – Strongly Disagree 2 – Disagree 3 – Neither Agree nor Disagree 4 – Agree 5 – Strongly Agree

HOW EFFECTIVE IS OUR BOARD AT ESTABLISHING WRITTEN CRITERIA AND QUALIFICATIONS FOR BOARD MEMBERS?	CIRCLE YOUR ANSWER
We have a **"Board Member Annual Affirmation Statement"** (or similar document) that summarizes the roles and responsibilities of board members, including future board meeting dates—and the board member's affirmation that he or she will be in attendance.	1 2 3 4 5
With crystal clarity, we explain the three distinct hats of board service: ✓ The Governance Hat ✓ The Volunteer Hat ✓ The Participant Hat	1 2 3 4 5
We are also crystal clear about a board member's charitable giving expectations (if any).	1 2 3 4 5

Use this template to create your own "Board Member Annual Affirmation Statement" so current board members, and board prospects, understand—with crystal clarity—their roles and responsibilities.

> YOUR LOGO AND CONTACT INFORMATION HERE

Board Member Annual Affirmation Statement
(Approved by the Board on _____, 2019)

"ANY ENTERPRISE IS BUILT BY WISE PLANNING, BECOMES STRONG THROUGH COMMON SENSE,
AND PROFITS WONDERFULLY BY KEEPING ABREAST OF THE FACTS."
Proverbs 24:3-4, *The Living Bible*

OUR GOVERNANCE VISION. It is our expectation and hope that in future years, the members of the Board of Directors of XYZ Ministries would sense such a high calling to their roles and responsibilities—and have such a vision for the potential of serving others—that they would give the highest priority (as defined by our Board Policies Manual) in the use of their charitable time and resources to XYZ Ministries during their three-year term of service on the board.

THE ROLES AND RESPONSIBILITIES OF BOARD MEMBERS

The full description of board member roles is listed in our Board Policies Manual. In summary, we desire to make <u>spiritually discerning governance and policy decisions</u> in these key areas:

1) **People.** We are accountable for the hiring, inspiring, guiding, evaluating, and the supporting of our CEO.

2) **Policies.** We focus on governance (as defined in the Board Policies Manual) and our stewarding and accountability process for the ministry (and our board) in the key areas of mission, vision, values, B.H.A.G. (Big HOLY Audacious Goal), strategy, strategic plan (at least three years), and the annual organizational goals; plus the CEO's three to five "Annual S.M.A.R.T. Goals" (which are Specific, Measurable, Achievable, Realistic and Time-related).

3) **Strategy.** We agree with Ram Charan's statement in *Owning Up: The 14 Questions Every Board Member Needs to Ask*, that we want our board to <u>own</u> the strategy, but not necessarily create it. He writes, "There is nothing more important for a CEO than having the right strategy and right choice of goals, and for the board, the right strategy is second only to having the right CEO."[10]

4) **Legal and Financial Due Diligence.** We take very seriously our fiduciary, legal and spiritual responsibilities as trustees of the ministry and we ensure that we are in compliance with all legal, financial, and governmental requirements, as described in our Board Policies Manual. These include, but are not limited to, policy oversight of the annual budget, cash flow, cash reserves, risk management, audits, ECFA-accreditation standards, CEO compensation, and other areas.

5) **Generous Giving.** We invite spiritually discerning and qualified men and women to serve on our board who are already in the "Generous Givers Circle," as defined in our Board Policies Manual—and who through example and influence, will encourage others to give generously to our ministry.

This document will be used two ways:

1) We will ask <u>current board members</u> to review and sign this—and affirm their commitment to XYZ Ministries annually.

2) We will ask <u>prospective board members</u> to review this in advance of their commitment to serve—and then upon their election, to sign the affirmation annually.

---

[10] Ram Charan, *Owning Up: The 14 Questions Every Board Member Needs to* Ask (San Francisco: Jossey-Bass, 2009), 68.

The 3 Hats of a Board Member

☑ GOVERNANCE HAT
All board members wear their "Governance" hats at board meetings. Here we seek to spiritually discern God's voice together as we steward the direction of the ministry in God-honoring ways.

☑ VOLUNTEER HAT
Contrary to what your experience may have been on other boards, here we affirm that "volunteering is optional—and is gifts-based and passion-driven." If your primary reason for serving on our board is to expand your current volunteer role or a future volunteer role, you might be more fulfilled giving more time and energy to that volunteer role—and *not* serve on the board. We see these two hats as distinct and separate.

When a board member does wear a volunteer hat (remember—it's optional), we remind that person to leave his or her "Governance" hat back in the boardroom! We know you won't "power up" as a board member when you're volunteering—and that you will respect the volunteer lines of authority by working with the appropriate staff or volunteer supervisor. And, of course, we know you will also refrain from bringing volunteer issues into the board meeting so other board members won't be tempted to micro-manage staff functions and neglect board functions.

☑ PARTICIPANT HAT
The "Participant" hat (as you'll note in this document) includes those events in our calendar year that we expect board members to attend. While you may be introduced as a board member here, these events are not board meetings and so, once again, it would be inappropriate for you to wear your "Governance" hat at these events. In advance, we may ask for your help in some way at an event and so you might be called upon to also wear your "Volunteer" hat. Thanks!

For more information on the 3 Board Hats, download and view:

ECFA Governance Toolbox Series No. 2: Balancing Board Roles
Understanding the 3 Board Hats: Governance, Volunteer, Participant

www.ecfa.org/toolbox

Session 1 ◆ Balancing Board Roles

Your Name: _____

XYZ MINISTRIES
Board Member Annual Affirmation Statement

MY COMMITMENT.

☐ **Yes!** I affirm my high commitment and generous use of my *time, talent and treasures* for the purposes of kingdom advancement through the work of XYZ Ministries. I believe God has called me to serve and I accept these roles, responsibilities and privileges with joy and enthusiasm.

Term of office: January 1, 2020 to December 31, 2022 (3 years)

Board Members Wear 3 Hats:
☑ Governance Hat
☑ Volunteer Hat (based on your strengths, social style and spiritual gifts)
☑ Participant Hat (participation at ministry events and fundraising dinners, etc.)

◆ GOVERNANCE HAT:

Circle: Yes or No

Yes No   1. I affirm the XYZ Ministries Statement of Faith.

Yes No   2. I affirm I will serve faithfully on the XYZ Ministries Board of Directors, confident that I have the enthusiastic affirmation of my family (and my employer, if required) along with their understanding of the commitments I am making in the use of my time, talent and treasure.

Yes No   3. I affirm I will pray regularly for XYZ Ministries, the CEO, the staff, and the Board of Directors.

Yes No. 4. I affirm I am <u>highly committed</u> to attending the scheduled meetings of the board and committees and understand that the cost of transportation, hotel, and non-scheduled meals will be my responsibility. I will also participate in the regularly scheduled telephone conference calls. *(See the attached list for future board meetings.)*

Yes No   5. I affirm that during my three-year term on the board I will arrange my giving priorities so that I am able to be a <u>generous giver</u> to XYZ Ministries, recognizing that major donors, foundations and other donors have the expectation that the XYZ Ministries Board of Directors will be part of the "most highly committed" group of donors.
    Note: "Generous giving" does not mean that our board members must be wealthy. Instead, when at all possible, we encourage each board member to prioritize XYZ Ministries so it is one of the "Top-3" ministries for an individual's annual giving. (See the Board Policies Manual for more details.)

Yes No   6. I affirm that, as I'm able, I will seek to influence my colleagues, my organization/company, major donors and foundations to be generous givers to our ministry.

Session 1 ◆ Balancing Board Roles

Yes No.   7. I affirm that I am an active attender and participant in my local church and am committed to a spiritual journey of becoming a fully devoted follower of Christ.

Yes No   8. I affirm that I will carefully consider opportunities for service on various board committees and will accept such assignments, as I am able. Note: current standing committees of the board are:
        a) Executive Committee
        b) Finance and Audit Review Committee
        c) Governance Committee

Yes No   9. I affirm that if I am unable or unwilling to continue to serve, prepare for and attend meetings, and execute my responsibilities as a member of the Board of Directors of XYZ Ministries, I will resign my position so that the board may have the benefit of the full support and committed time, talent and treasure of an active board member.

Yes No   10. Other: _____

◆ VOLUNTEER HAT:

Circle: Yes or No

Yes No   1. I understand that while I am encouraged to serve as a volunteer of XYZ Ministries, <u>such service is separate from my roles and responsibilities as a board member</u>. I understand that volunteer service is optional, but should I volunteer, the organization will seek to place me in a volunteer role that leverages my spiritual gifts, strengths and social styles.

Yes No   2. I affirm that should I serve as a volunteer, I will respect the lines of authority and accountability and not inappropriately bring my "Volunteer" hat ideas, suggestions, issues or recommendations to the board—but I will work directly with the staff person or volunteer that supervises or coordinates my volunteer work.

Yes No   3. As a XYZ Ministries volunteer, I affirm I will prayerfully consider other opportunities for volunteer service, including:
- Representing the organization at meetings and events
- Serving at an event
- Serving on an ad hoc task force or committee
- Joining the CEO in meetings with potential donors
- Other: _____

Yes No   4. Other: _____

Session 1 ◆ Balancing Board Roles

◆ PARTICIPANT HAT:

Circle: Yes or No

Yes No 1. I understand that as board member, I am expected to attend selected events each year as a participant—and that, as much as possible, those calendar dates will be announced a year in advance. I also understand that married board members will be highly encouraged to involve their spouses in many of these events.

Yes No 2. I affirm I will aggressively encourage others to become involved with XYZ Ministries and invite at least [circle: 3, 5, 10, ___] people new to the ministry to participate in one or more events each year, when possible.

Yes No 3. I will seek to participate in at least one major ministry event each year (such as the Annual Workshop) at my own expense. I understand that board members will receive a _____% discount on registration fees for this event. I also understand I may be asked to volunteer at this event.

Yes No 4. Other: _____

1 Corinthians 4:2 reminds us that to be a steward it is required that one be found trustworthy. Before God, it is my desire to be faithful in stewarding the important work of XYZ Ministries!

Signed: _____ **Date** _____

Print Name: _____

CONFLICT OF INTEREST DISCLOSURE LETTER AND POLICY

☑ **Two Options:**

❏ 1. Visit the ECFA Knowledge Center, www.ECFA.org, for a conflict of interest template.

❏ 2. Download and view:

ECFA Governance Toolbox Series No. 3:
Conflicts of Interest - Addressing Board and Organizational Conflicts of Interest

Avoiding Trouble, Trouble, Trouble with Related-Party Transactions!

http://www.ecfa.org/Toolbox

Board of Directors - XYZ Ministries

CONFLICT OF INTEREST DISCLOSURE LETTER AND POLICY

[insert pages here]

2020 Board Meeting Schedule (Updated: July 15, 2019)

Year 2020	Day/Time	Location	Agenda
Meeting #1 Date: _____	Tuesday 2 – 4 p.m.	Telephone Conference Call	• 2019 Financial Reports/Budget Review • 2020 Financial Reports (2 months) • 2020 Budget (final review) • Committee Reports • Executive Director's "State of the Organization" report for 2019 and 2020 • Strategic Plan update
Meeting #2 Date: _____	Thursday 12 noon – Lunch 1 – 5 p.m. 5:30 p.m. Optional Dinner (spouses invited)	TBD	• Financial Reports (4 months) • Committee Reports • Executive Director's S.M.A.R.T. Goals update • Leading Indicators update • Nominating Committee Report
Meeting #3 **Board Retreat** Date: _____	**BOARD RETREAT** **Thursday 4 p.m. to Friday 2 p.m.**	TBD	• Financial Report (7 months) • Strategic Plan (2021 - 2023) – Draft 1 (BHAG, Primary Customer, Mission, Strategies, Business Model, Development Plan etc.) • Nominating Committee recommendations on board prospects
Meeting #4 Date: _____	Thursday 12 noon – Lunch 1 - 5 p.m. 5:30 p.m. Dinner (spouses invited)	TBD	• Welcome New Board Members • Financial Reports (10 months) • 2021 Annual Plan, Calendar, Leading Indicators and Executive Director's 2021 S.M.A.R.T. Goals • 2021 Preliminary Budget • Executive Director's Performance Review (based on 2020 S.M.A.R.T. Goals) • Board Governance Committee Report • Appointment of Auditor

2020 "Participant Hat" Expectations for Board Members (Updated: _____, 2019)

Date	Day/Time	Location	Event (*Required Attendance)
			*
			*
			(Optional):
			(Optional):

2021 Board Meeting Schedule (Updated: _____, 2019) - Proposed

Year 2021	Day/Time	Location	Agenda

RESOURCES:

For more help on using this tool, order:

> **ECFA Governance Toolbox Series No. 1: Recruiting Board Members**
> Leveraging the 4 Phases of Board Recruitment
> Cultivation ▶ Recruitment ▶ Orientation ▶ Engagement
> **www.ecfa.org/toolbox**

**Engage Your Board at Every Meeting
With More Governance Help and Resources!**

Visit ECFA.org/toolbox to order additional titles in the ECFA Governance Toolbox Series.

ECFA

440 West Jubal Early Drive, Suite 100
Winchester, VA 22601 USA
Telephone: (540) 535-0103
information@ECFA.org - www.ECFA.org

© Copyright, 2012. ECFA - All Rights Reserved.
May not be reproduced or rebroadcast in any form
without permission from ECFA.

Session 1 ◆ Balancing Board Roles

❑ 4. BEST PRACTICE WHEN WEARING THE GOVERNANCE HAT:
Annually Affirm the "CEO Annual S.M.A.R.T. Goals and Monthly Dashboard Report"

S.M.A.R.T. GOALS DEFINED
Annual S.M.A.R.T. Goals must be Specific, Measurable, Achievable, Realistic, and Time-related.

☑ **Specific.** What results will be achieved?

☑ **Measurable.** Is the exact target and finish line crystal clear? (You'll know when to celebrate because everyone will agree the goal was reached.)

☑ **Achievable:** Is it pie-in-the-sky? Has this goal ever been achieved before—by anyone?

☑ **Realistic:** Is the goal rooted in reality and aligned with adequate resources? Does the team agree? Has your spiritual discernment process confirmed this? Note: "The actual achievement of audacious goals is very uncommon."[11]

☑ **Time-related:** Is there a specific target date (not a target month)? (Instead of generalizing with "3rd Quarter," commit to "Sept. 30, 2019.")

SMART GOALS AND *NOT-SO-SMART GOALS*:

S.M.A.R.T. GOALS	SPECIFIC	MEASURABLE	ACHIEVABLE	REALISTIC	TIME-RELATED
■ ***NOT-SO-SMART GOALS***					
1) Plan the best annual meeting event on the planet!					
2) Increase the number of major donors giving $5 billion or more.	✓	✓			
3) Conduct a client satisfaction survey by Sept. 30, 2018.		✓	✓	✓	✓
4) Launch the XYZ Program as soon as possible in numerous cities.					
5) To raise $50,000, ask every donor to give an extra $10 this month.	✓	✓			✓
■ **SMART GOALS**					
1) Survey annual meeting participants on 5 key factors by May 15.	✓	✓	✓	✓	✓
2) Increase the number of major donors by 15% by Oct. 25.	✓	✓	✓	✓	✓
3) Score 4.2 or better on our client satisfaction survey by 9/25/19.	✓	✓	✓	✓	✓
4) Launch the XYZ Program in these 25 cities (see list) by 6/30/19.	✓	✓	✓	✓	✓
5) *Write a goal here:*	✓	✓	✓	✓	✓

---

[11] Busby and Pearson, *Lessons From the Nonprofit Boardroom*, 194. Read "Lesson 37: Don't Stretch Credulity With BHAGs and Stretch Goals."

Session 1 ◆ Balancing Board Roles

SAMPLE TEMPLATE: MONTHLY DASHBOARD REPORT[12]
(COLOR-CODE EACH MONTHLY PROGRESS REPORT)*

S.M.A.R.T. Goals are: ➔ **S**pecific, **M**easurable, **A**chievable, **R**ealistic, and **T**ime-related.

ABC Ministry – CEO Monthly Dashboard Report (2020)
Annual TOP-5 SMART GOALS for Jane Doe
Monthly Update to be submitted to Board of Directors by the 15th of each month.
These FY2020 TOP-5 SMART GOALS were approved by the Board of Directors on Dec. 15, 2019.

FY2020 - 3 Months January 1 – March 31, 2020 *Updated on April 15, 2020 by Jane Doe*	Target Date	Monthly Update 3-Month Report Ending 3/31/2020
1. Revenue and Expenses. Achieve the year-end net income goal of $40,000, based on revenue of $500,000 and expense of $460,000.	12/31/20	• On target
2. Operating Reserves. Increase operating reserves from $114,000 to $154,000 (equivalent to 4 months of the FY2020 expense budget).	12/31/20	• We are now forecasting just 2 months of reserve by year-end. Finance Comm. will review a revised "Plan B."
3. Board Member Recruitment. Assist the board with cultivating up to five new board prospects for terms beginning on Jan. 1, 2021.	9/30/20	• **Due to the Project XX crisis, our board chair and I have not invested any time on this.**
4. Three-Year Rolling Strategic Plan: 2021-2023. Based on board feedback, recommend the final version of the 2021-2023 Strategic Plan to the board.	9/15/20	• Board will review at the September board meeting
5. Vision 2025 Resource Center. Implement the Phase 1 Pilot Program of the Vision 2025 Virtual Resource Center, including the cultivation, recruitment, orientation and engagement of 2 state coordinators, 10 area coordinators and 50 local church ambassadors.	10/31/20	• On target! Mike Pate has agreed to be our State of Hawaii coordinator! And…17 new coordinators have also become "Level 3 Donors."

↑ *COLOR-CODE EACH BOX BASED ON THE MONTHLY UPDATE.

COLOR CODES:	Green ON TARGET	Yellow CAUTION	Red ALERT!

> "Goals are over-arching and should be few in number.
> **If you have more than five goals, you have none.**
> You're simply spreading yourself too thin."[13]
>
> Peter Drucker

---

[12] Busby and Pearson, *ECFA Tools and Templates for Effective Board Governance*
[13] Peter F. Drucker, Frances Hesselbein, and Joan Snyder Kuhl, *Peter Drucker's Five Most Important Questions: Enduring Wisdom for Today's Leaders* (Hoboken, NJ: John Wiley and Sons, Inc., 2015), 5-6.

SESSION 2

Improving and Enriching the Board Experience by Focusing on Board Recruitment

- ☑ Cultivation
- ☑ Recruitment
- ☑ Orientation
- ☑ Engagement

SESSION 2:
Improving and Enriching the Board Experience by Focusing on Board Recruitment

Cultivation➔Recruitment➔Orientation➔Engagement
How do ministries recruit board prospects and engage them as faithful and fruitful board members?

☑ **HEALTHY GOVERNANCE CHECKLIST**
CCCA Thriving Boards ◆ Growing Healthy, Effective Boards

#2. NEW BOARD MEMBERS ARE RECRUITED *SLOWLY*...WITH DISCERNMENT.
❑ CULTIVATION: We have written board member criteria and pray before prospecting.
❑ RECRUITMENT: We "date" prospects before proposing marriage and guide them into the circles of involvement.
❑ ORIENTATION: We have a written new board member orientation process that spans about six months.
❑ ENGAGEMENT: We have high expectations (in writing) of all board members and leverage their "3 Powerful S's."

IN THIS SESSION:

❑ 1. <u>VIDEO</u>: The 4 Phases of Board Recruitment and Engagement

❑ 2. <u>RESOURCE</u>: The 7 Steps for Recruiting Board Members

❑ 3. <u>INSIGHT</u>: Why Focusing on Board Recruitment Will Enrich Everyone's Board Experience

THE BOARD BUCKET CORE COMPETENCY

"We believe that board members must sense God's call to serve on the board of directors. We invest time in cultivating, recruiting, orienting and engaging board members in their strategic role as stewards of our organization. The first step in organizational sustainability is to inspire board members to be highly committed and generous partners in ministry."[14]

---

[14] John Pearson, *Mastering the Management Buckets: 20 Critical Competencies for Leading Your Business or Nonprofit* (Ventura, CA: Regal, 2008), 191-200.

Session 2 ◆ Recruiting Board Members

❑ 1. VIDEO: The 4 Phases of Board Recruitment and Engagement

❑ ECFA Governance Toolbox Series No. 1: Recruiting Board Members
Leveraging the 4 Phases of Cultivation, Recruitment, Orientation, Engagement

www.ecfa.org/toolbox

➜ Contact CCCA Thriving Boards for access code: ☐

Each Toolbox includes:
- ❑ Online video
- ❑ *Board Member Read-and-Engage Viewing Guide*
- ❑ *Facilitator Guide*
- ❑ Access to tools, templates, and resources on hidden webpage

DOWNLOAD:
- ❑ *Board Member Annual Affirmation Statement* (sample template - identifying the "3 Hats of a Board Member") – see Session 1.
- ❑ *Board Nominee Orientation Binder* (Table of Contents) – see following pages.
- ❑ Resources on "The 3 Powerful S's" (Strengths, Social Styles, and Spiritual Gifts)

ECFA Tools and Templates for Effective Board Governance: Time-Saving Solutions for Your Board, by Dan Busby and John Pearson

➜ **Note!** This resource will also provide access to the tools included in this session (including access to Word documents)—so you can customize these tools for your board's unique use.

Session 2 ◆ Recruiting Board Members

VIDEO NOTES: THE 4 PHASES OF BOARD RECRUITMENT AND ENGAGEMENT

If you don't plan to engage board members—don't waste your time recruiting them!

❑ 1. Cultivation

❑ 2. Recruitment

❑ 3. Orientation

❑ 4. Engagement

Board Member Orientation: The Concise and Complete Guide to Nonprofit Board Service
by Michael E. Batts[15]

See Chapter 7, "The Liability of Board Members"

Lessons From the Nonprofit Boardroom: 40 Insights for Better Board Meetings, Second Edition
by Dan Busby and John Pearson[16]

See Lesson 34, "Envision Your Best Board Member Orientation Ever"

---

[15] Michael E. Batts, *Board Member Orientation: The Concise and Complete Guide to Nonprofit Board Service* (Orlando: Accountability Press, 2011), 47-51.
[16] Busby and Pearson, *Lessons From the Nonprofit Boardroom*, 178-183.

Session 2 ◆ Recruiting Board Members

WORKSHEET: The 4 Phases of Board Recruitment and Engagement

☑ In each row, check the box that best describes how effective your board is in these four phases of board recruitment and engagement.

THE 4 PHASES OF BOARD RECRUITMENT AND ENGAGEMENT	1 VERY INEFFECTIVE	2 INEFFECTIVE	3 NEITHER EFFECTIVE NOR INEFFECTIVE	4 EFFECTIVE	5 VERY EFFECTIVE
1. CULTIVATION ❑ Prayer List ❑ Board Member Criteria ❑ 18- to 36-month plan					
2. RECRUITMENT ❑ Board Nominee Orientation Binder ❑ Board Member Annual Affirmation Statement ❑ Board Roles and Responsibilities ❑ Recruitment Strategy					
3. ORIENTATION ❑ Purposeful New Member Orientation Plan (6 months) ❑ Orientation Feedback Plan					
4. ENGAGEMENT ❑ Preserving and Advancing the Mission ❑ Leveraging the 3 Powerful S's (Strengths, Spiritual Gifts, Social Styles) of Each Member ❑ Customized Annual BHAGs for Each Board Member[17]					

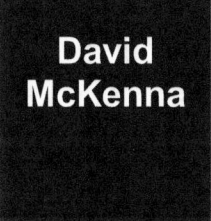

David McKenna

"If board members took an oath of office, we would first swear to 'preserve and advance the mission of the organization.' In almost the same breath, we would then pledge to 'accept the responsibility for the election of the CEO as our solemn duty and sacred trust.'"[18]

---

[17] The acronym, "BHAG," was popularized by Jim Collins in his book, *Built to Last*, and is defined as a "Big Hairy Audacious Goal." Many ministry organizations prefer to use the term "Big HOLY Audacious Goal."

[18] David L. McKenna, *Stewards of a Sacred Trust: CEO Selection, Transition and Development for Boards of Christ-centered Organizations* (Winchester, VA: ECFAPress, 2010), 17.

❏ 2. RESOURCE: THE 7 STEPS FOR RECRUITING BOARD MEMBERS

7 Steps for Recruiting Board Members
Excerpted, by permission, from Chapter 14, The Board Bucket, in *Mastering the Management Buckets: 20 Critical Competencies for Leading Your Business or Nonprofit*.[19]

① **RECRUIT** for passion—not position.
② **PRAY** before prospecting.
③ **DATE** before proposing!
④ **INSPIRE** your prospect to give generously.
⑤ **PROPOSE** marriage.
⑥ **CONTINUE** dating!
⑦ **LEAVE** a legacy.

If you work in a large for-profit company, you may not have relationships or influence with your corporate board. But sometime in your career, you'll likely be invited to serve on a church or nonprofit board. This chapter on THE BOARD BUCKET, *the first of seven buckets in the* CORPORATE *arena, is written both for church and nonprofit leaders and their current and prospective board members.*

Peter Drucker said that all boards have one thing in common—they do not function! That may be your experience too. So, while the content of this bucket is focused on the nonprofit world, you'll find excellent resources at the end of this chapter that will be helpful for both for-profit and nonprofit organizations.

* * *

One day way while Jesus was mentoring his disciples, he smiled (tongue-in-cheek) and said, "Show me the money!"

Actually, he said, "Show me your heart." Well...in reality, he said "For where your treasure is, there your heart will be also." (Matthew 6:21 NIV)

As we discussed in THE DONOR BUCKET, this is one of the most profound stewardship principles in Scripture, yet it is rarely practiced where it matters most—with board members of churches and nonprofit Christian organizations.

These arresting words from Jesus would look good on a t-shirt. President Bill Clinton should have said it this way, "It's the heart, stupid!"

The heart issue is the foundational building block for the four stages of building a board: cultivation, recruitment, orientation and engagement.

---

[19] Pearson, *Mastering the Management Buckets*, 191-200.

Session 2 ◆ Recruiting Board Members

While there are numerous balls in THE BOARD BUCKET, there are seven key balls—best practices—for recruiting exceptional board members in Christian organizations and churches. It's the first step toward effectiveness and if you ignore or short-cut any of these six steps, you'll pay for it sooner or later. At the end of this chapter, you'll also find a brief list of topics and board resources, if you want to go deeper into this bucket. But first things first. Let's get the right board members on the bus.

 BALL #1:

Recruit for Passion—Not Position.
Invite the already convinced zealots!

Recruit board members for their passion—not their position. Don't swallow the board myth that says you need a CPA, an attorney, a pastor and a fundraiser on your board. People in those positions make great volunteers, but might be less-than-loyal, uncommitted board members.

Instead, recruit highly committed people, with board governance skills, who are zealots for your ministry—and have already demonstrated multiple times their high passion for your mission.

If you need a volunteer, recruit a volunteer. If you need a board member, recruit a board member.

 BALL #2:

Pray Before Prospecting
Why settle for second best?

Right now—before you finish this chapter—begin your *Top 50 Prospects Prayer List*. Effective CEOs, senior pastors, and development officers know that it takes up to 36 months to bring exceptional board prospects into the board circle.

Jim Brown, author of *The Imperfect Board Member*, writes, "The problem is, most board cultures are developed by default, not by design."

Change that! The Lord wants you to have an extraordinary board. Imagine the potential when you energize exceptional board members who give spiritual oversight and excellent governance to your God-given mission.

Why settle for second best? Why recruit untested, uncommitted good candidates when—with prayer and hard work—the Lord could bless you with a sterling board team?

 BALL #3:

Date Before Proposing!
Bring board prospects inside the circle of involvement.

Thoughtful adults don't propose marriage on the first date. Effective CEOs don't propose board service to "B List" prospects. Think of this as a 36-month dating experience. But don't mention marriage (board service) up front.

39 | Thriving Boards Workbook ◆ 4th Edition

As you pray through the process, slowly bring the prospect inside the circles of involvement. Today, he or she may be unfamiliar with your ministry, so add them to your mailing list and invite them to an event. Test their interest with a volunteer role. Just like in dating, continue to evaluate over many months if your prospect demonstrates growing interest, and ultimately passion, for your important mission.

If Cliff turns out to be a lousy volunteer, drop him! You've saved yourself from marrying a lousy board member. If Susan gives 110 percent and recruits friends and families beyond expectation—you've got a live one! Keep dating!

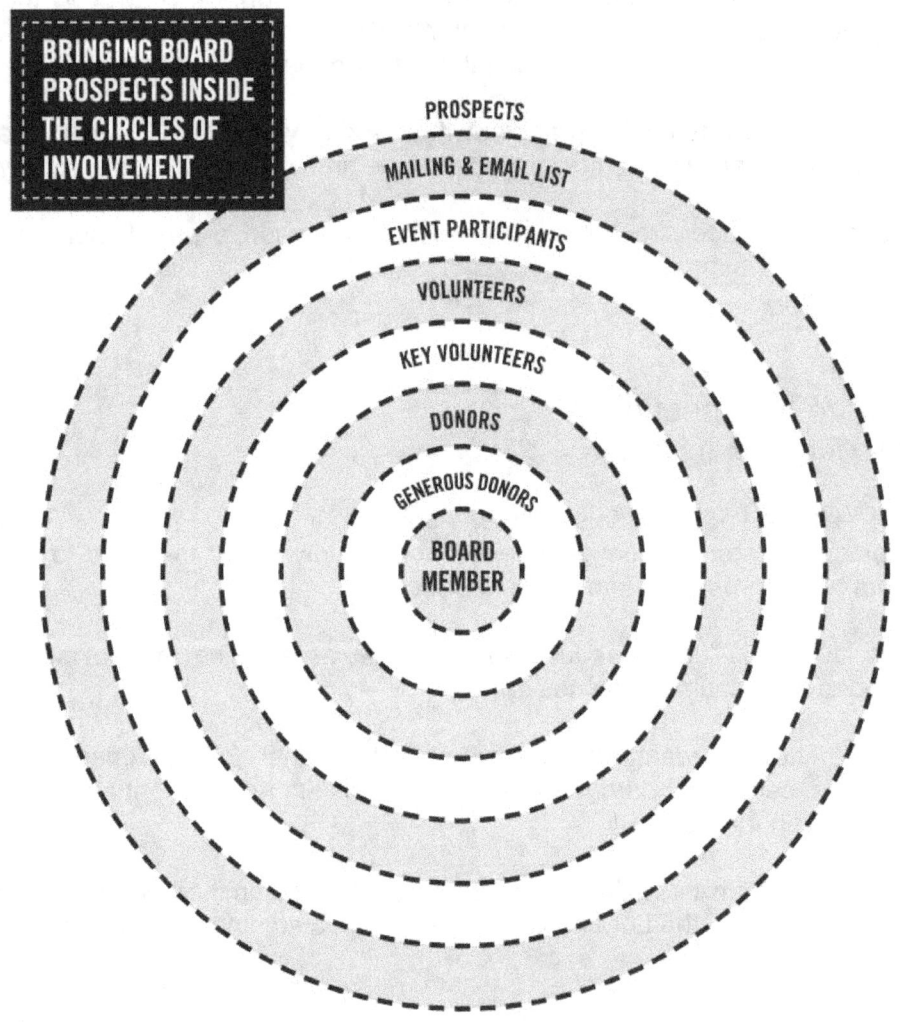

BALL #4:

Inspire Your Prospect to Give Generously
Model and teach The Treasure Principle.

When you're sharing these principles with other team members and board members, take out Ball #1 in THE DONOR BUCKET and review the principles of generous giving (your heart follows your money). Talk about the biblical values in Randy Alcorn's book, *The Treasure Principle*. The idea of extravagant generosity is not just for board recruitment. It is not a fundraising gimmick. It is a core value for the fully devoted follower of Christ. Don't settle for second best when you're "dating" a board prospect.

Recruit intentionally, with generosity in mind, and you'll breathe new life into your ministry. As you "date" board prospects, challenge them spiritually to become generous givers to your mission. Explain why you need a team of highly committed donors who demonstrate through their giving where their hearts are.

Without waving the carrot of board service (you haven't proposed yet), inspire your prospect (and the spouse, if the person is married) with the opportunity to make your ministry one of their top three annual giving priorities. That's the definition of a generous giver for your ministry.

If a prospect says no, that's OK. You've discovered where his or her heart is—before the wedding. (He or she may already be highly committed, even a generous giver, to two or three other ministries.) That's the good news—you took the temperature on their passion before you popped the question.

Here's the bad news—there are thousands of nonprofit CEOs that have "married" board members way too soon—and the commitment, the passion, the giving and the heart never followed. Save yourself the agony and do it right by starting your prospect prayer list today.

BALL #5:

Propose Marriage
Once your prospects have moved into the generous giving circle, then it's time to invite them onto the board.

You'll know when it's time to propose marriage (board service). The prospect will have already demonstrated a high level of commitment, all the time moving towards the center of the involvement circle. They will meet all of the previously established board criteria. Plus, the Lord will confirm it to you and your nominating committee.

But again, here's a reminder. Never, never, never invite anyone to serve on your board who is not already a generous giver to your ministry. In my consulting work, I've found I can never say this too many times.

The board candidate does not need to be wealthy—just generous. Generally that means that during this person's term of service on the board, he or she will make your ministry their first, second or third highest annual giving priority. No exceptions. Remember, Jesus said, "For where your treasure is, there your heart will be also."

Where this core value is practiced, board members attest to the remarkable culture change that happens on the board. Passionate, highly committed board members—who follow their money with their heart—become incredible zealots for your mission. Wow!

So when you have prospects that are highly committed to your church or ministry—and meet all the board criteria—pop the question and invite them to serve on your board.

Give them a full ministry briefing, in advance of asking for their decision. Many organizations provide prospects with a Board Nominee Orientation Binder, filled with helpful background information (staff salaries, board minutes, financials—soup to nuts) so the nominee can make an informed and prayerful decision about board service.

Moving Board Donors to Generous Givers

Do you have people on your board today who are not generous givers? Your CEO and/or board chair should plan a one-on-one appointment with each board member. Invite each person to lunch or dinner and mentor your board member on what Jesus taught about giving and why a totally committed board member is so critical. Then ask your board members for their gifts and their hearts.

WORKSHEET: The Generous Giving Continuum

☑ Check the box that best represents your current board policy on board member giving—and where you'd like it to be in 12 months:

The Generous Giving Continuum	1 We do not believe giving ought to be a criteria for board service.	2 It's the elephant on the table. Our board needs to talk about it—and make a policy decision.	3 We discussed this and have decided NOT to make a board policy on giving.	4 By policy, all board members must be donors of record, but not necessarily at the Top-3 level.	5 By policy, all board members must prioritize their giving to our ministry at the Top-3 level.
Our board's current policy is:					
In 12 months, I'd like to see our policy be:					

"FOR WHERE YOUR TREASURE IS,
THERE YOUR HEART WILL BE ALSO."
MATTHEW 6:21 NIV

 BALL #6:
Continue Dating!
Help your board members hone their board governance competencies.

The wedding (board member installation) is only the beginning. Ensure that all board members hone their board competencies regularly. Most will bring a diversity of expectations into your board room. They'll also bring the delightful dysfunctional baggage they've picked up from other board experiences.

Use your board meetings, your conference calls, your mailings and at least one board retreat each year to help members become life-long learners on board best practices. Introduce them to board governance workshops, books, articles, websites and CDs. Invite resource people (consultants, other CEOs, professors, etc.) to train, motivate and inspire your board team. Bless your board members and they'll be a blessing to your ministry!

 BONUS BALL #7:
Leave a Legacy
Grow a great board!

Bob Andringa teaches that one of the greatest legacies a CEO can leave to an organization is a great board. He should know. As managing partner of The Andringa Group (TheAndringaGroup.com) and former president of the Council for Christian Colleges and Universities, Bob has consulted with more than 200 boards over the years. When he speaks or writes books on board governance, nonprofit leaders listen!

A Chinese proverb says that if you want one year of prosperity, grow grain. If you want 10 years of prosperity, grow trees. If you want 100 years of prosperity, grow people.

At this point in your management buckets journey, you may be on overload or just slightly overwhelmed with the CAUSE, COMMUNITY and CORPORATION buckets. You may have a growing list of "I know what I don't know." Don't despair. When you perfect the core competencies in the CORPORATION buckets, you then have the infrastructure for sustainability. Don't neglect THE BOARD BUCKET.

Another Chinese proverb reads, "The best time to plant a tree was twenty years ago. The second best time, is today." Start growing a great board today.

Bucket Bottom Line
When you are effective in THE BOARD BUCKET, it creates a remarkable ripple effect in THE DONOR BUCKET, THE RESULTS BUCKET, and THE VOLUNTEER BUCKET (to name a few). However, when you have low commitment and low passion among board members—and lackluster giving versus extravagant generosity—you will never fully recover and gain organizational momentum until you fix the problems in THE BOARD BUCKET.

BOARD OF DIRECTORS - BOARD NOMINEE ORIENTATION BINDER[20]

Table of Contents (3-ring binder, 31-tab format) – [Organization Name Here]

	INTRODUCTORY MATERIALS
1	Introduction from the Chairman of the Board of Directors
2	General Brochures, Publications, (eNewsletter, Website outline, etc.)
3	Historical Snapshot, Honors, Awards, Notable News Clippings
	BOARD OF DIRECTORS
4	Current Board Members (Mini-Bios), Committees, and Volunteer Structure
5	Board Member Annual Affirmation Statement, Calendar of Future Board Meetings, Board Member Application Form, and Biographical Sketch
6	Nomination and Election Procedures
7	Bylaws, Articles of Incorporation, etc.
8	Board Policies Manual (BPM)
9	Conflict of Interest Disclosure Letter
10	Former Board Members and Board Chairs
11	Board Meeting Agenda/Pages (of most recent meeting) – *sample*
12	Board Issues/Challenges for Next 3 Years, including: "Any skeletons in the boardroom closet?"
	FINANCE, BUDGET, IRS, ECFA REPORTS
13	Annual Budget
14	Current Financial Reports
15	Audited Financial Statements
16	ECFA Membership, Profile and Public Statistics
17	IRS Form 990 *(Return of Org. Exempt from Income Tax)*
	STRATEGIC PLAN AND METRICS
18	Rolling 3-Year Strategic Plan and Strategic Plan Placemat (one-page summary: 11" x17")
19	Annual Customer Satisfaction Surveys
20	CEO's Annual S.M.A.R.T. Goals and Board/CEO Accountability Process (Monthly Dashboard)
21	Leading Indicators/Key Performance Indicators (KPIs), Statistics (charts and graphs)
22	Our Answers to Peter Drucker's "Five Questions Every Nonprofit Organization Must Answer"
23	"Radar Issues" (1-page) – "Our Assumptions About the Next 3 Years"
	TEAM MEMBERS
24	Organizational Chart and Mini-Position Descriptions: Staff Contact Info
25	Team Member Mini-Bios; CEO Bio, CEO's Top-5 Strengths (StrengthsFinder.com)
26	Confidential Compensation Schedule
	DEVELOPMENT
27	Donor Development Program - Snapshot
28	Direct Mail, Campaign/Project, Brochure Samples
29	Development Program Annual and 3-Year Goals (and the fundraising role of board members)
	PROGRAMS AND SERVICES
30	Menu of Programs, Products, and Services for "Primary Customers" and "Supporting Customers" (and annual program evaluation process)
31	Other

---

[20] Busby and Pearson, *ECFA Tools and Templates for Effective Board Governance*

❑ 3. INSIGHT: WHY FOCUSING ON BOARD RECRUITMENT WILL ENRICH EVERYONE'S BOARD EXPERIENCE

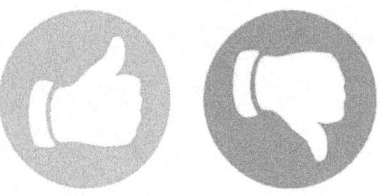

3 STATEMENTS	YES	NO	I DON'T KNOW!
❑ 1. DYSFUNCTION. We agree that… "There are no dysfunctional organizations, only dysfunctional boards."			
❑ 2. IMPROVEMENT. If we improve our current governance capabilities, it is more likely that high quality board prospects will be eager to consider board service.			
❑ 3. EXCELLENCE. If we believe that excellence in our governance honors God—and our board prospects sense this during the "dating" process—then it is more likely that board prospects will see board service as a holy calling and a sacred trust—and our board culture will thrive.			

"Frankly, I don't know why I called this meeting."

SESSION 3

Breakout...
With Your Coach

SESSION 3:
Breakout...With Your Coach

IN THIS SESSION:

❏ 1. BOOK: *Scaling Up*—A Quick Overview

❏ 2. TOOL: Healthy Governance Checklist—A Quick Overview

❏ 3. DISCUSSION OPTIONS: Your Coach Will Give You Discussion Options (if there's time)

Breakout Bonus (optional—if there's time!):

❏ 4. FACILITATION TOOLS: Use a Fresh Facilitation Tool at Your Next Board Meeting

NOTES:

❏ 1. BOOK: *SCALING UP*—A QUICK OVERVIEW

SCALING UP:
How a Few Companies Make It...and
Why the Rest Don't
Mastering the Rockefeller Habits 2.0[21]
by Verne Harnish

The author says there are three barriers to scaling up:
❏ 1. Leadership
❏ 2. Scalable infrastructure
❏ 3. Marketing

To overcome these barriers, he says you must master four fundamentals:
❏ 1. Leading People
❏ 2. Setting Strategy
❏ 3. Driving Execution
❏ 4. Managing Cash

In Thriving Boards, we'll recommend the role of the board and the role of the CEO/staff. Caution to Board Members! *Scaling Up* is primarily a resource for the CEO and the staff.

	Four Fundamentals	The CEO will:	The board will:
1	Leading People	❏ Lead the team	❏ Set board-level policy ❏ Lead the CEO
2	Setting Strategy	❏ Recommend and execute the strategy and the strategic plan	❏ Set board-level policy ❏ Own the strategy and the strategic plan
3	Driving Execution	❏ Drive all execution	❏ Set board-level policy ❏ Review plans, progress, KPIs[22], goals, and results ❏ Advise the CEO ❏ *Not* micromanage!
4	Managing Cash	❏ Recommend budgets ❏ Submit financial reports ❏ Build organizational sustainability	❏ Set board-level policy ❏ Review and approve budgets, financial reports, cash flow forecasts, operating reserves, spending limits, etc.

---

[21] Harnish, *Scaling Up*
[22] Read more on KPIs (Kept Promise Indicators) in *Scaling Up* on page 115. "...it's critical that you know how to measure daily whether you're keeping your promises."

Session 3 ◆ Breakout With Your Coach

❑ 2. TOOL: HEALTHY GOVERNANCE CHECKLIST—A QUICK OVERVIEW

FOR CEOs AND STAFF:

☑ *Rockefeller Habits Checklist*™

➜ **NOTE:** *Scaling Up* leverages the *Rockefeller Habits Checklist*™, 40 critical "habits" that the team must address in 10 major areas.

You can download a one-page copy of the *Rockefeller Habits Checklist*™ at the author's company website (including other tools) here: www.ScalingUp.com. You can also download it here: https://gazelles.com/static/resources/tools/en/RH_Checklist.pdf

Verne Harnish

"**WARNING: You'll drive everyone in the organization crazy if you implement all of these habits at one time.** The key is focusing on one or two each quarter, giving everyone roughly 24 to 36 months to install these simple, yet powerful routines. Then it's a process of continually refreshing them as the company scales up." (See page 15 and read why habits are "routines that set you free!")[23]

FOR BOARD MEMBERS:

☑ *HEALTHY GOVERNANCE CHECKLIST*

➜ **NEW!** For the 4th Edition of the *Thriving Boards Workbook*, the coaches and presenters are inviting your input and feedback on the first draft of this new document, *Healthy Governance Checklist.*

What are the Top-40 or Top-50 (or maybe Top-100) critical tasks/affirmations that should be on the *CCCA Thriving Boards Healthy Governance Checklist*?

☑ **HEALTHY GOVERNANCE CHECKLIST**
CCCA Thriving Boards ◆ Growing Healthy, Effective Boards

#1. EVERY BOARD MEMBER UNDERSTANDS THE THREE BOARD HATS.
❑ The GOVERNANCE hat is policy-oriented and worn only during board meetings (and never when volunteering).
❑ The VOLUNTEER hat is optional and is not worn during board meetings.
❑ The PARTICIPANT hat is worn at "required attendance" events for board members (identified a year in advance).
❑ *The Board Member Annual Affirmation Statement* details the roles and responsibilities of board members (based on the three hats) and this document is signed and affirmed by all board members every January.

NOTE: See pages 10-12 for the complete "Healthy Governance Checklist."

---

[23] Harnish, *Scaling Up*, 15.

❑ 3. DISCUSSION OPTIONS:
Your Coach Will Give You Discussion Options (if there's time)

TOPIC	NOTES:
#1. "Our Top-5 Strategic Next Steps" worksheet ✓ How to get the most mileage out of this tool.	
#2. Review your Organizational Profile ✓ Any surprises? ✓ What are your strengths?	
#3. Review the Pre-Session Survey results ✓ Compare your results to the combined results of all cohort participants	
#4. Browse this resource: ✓ ECFA Tools and Templates for Effective Board Governance ✓ Select one tool to begin using this month!	

Breakout Bonus (if there's time!):
❏ **4. FACILITATION TOOLS: USE A FRESH FACILITATION TOOL AT YOUR NEXT MEETING**

Try one of these engagement exercises with your board:

❏ **1. Around-the-room** (60-second responses)

❏ **2. Partners** (Person A talks, Person B listens and reports)

❏ **3. Triads** (Person A poses a question, Persons B and C suggest answers. *Person A smiles and says thank you—but that's all!*)

❏ **4. Stand and Declare!** (everyone stands, then each person, clockwise, "declares" *briefly*; and takes a seat after he/she shares)

❏ **5. Four Corners Topics** (go to the corner where the topic interests you). Example: SWOT exercise with a flipchart in each corner:
- ✓ Corner #1: Strengths
- ✓ Corner #2: Weaknesses
- ✓ Corner #3: Opportunities
- ✓ Corner #4: Threats

➔Note: Read *Scaling Up's* insights on where senior leaders should focus their time when addressing strategy.[24]

"HEAVY-LIFTING" OPTIONAL TOPICS FOR THIS SESSION WITH YOUR COACH:

TOPIC	NOTES:
#1. A new board best practice we launched in the last 24 months:	
#2. Can anyone suggest a solution to this board challenge?	

---

[24] Harnish, *Scaling Up*, 12-13. The author recommends that managers work on the SWOT analysis, but senior teams should focus energies on SWT (Strengths, Weaknesses, and Trends).

Session 3 ◆ Breakout With Your Coach

TOPIC	NOTES:
#3. My "go-to" resource for board best practices is:	
#4. I would have greater joy in my role if I could change one thing (not having to do with $):	
#5. Am I crazy? Our board is stuck on this **One Big Issue** that is preventing us from doing this: _____. Any suggestions (other than therapy)?	
#6. We need new blood on our board. Any ideas?	
#7. Here's how I would define "our reality" as a board today. But…here's my vision for the next 12 months.	

SESSION 4

Leading From a Healthy Governance Model

Creating Clarity and Alignment

John Carver

"GOVERNING BY POLICY means governing out of policy in the sense that no board activity takes place without reference to policies. Most resolutions in board meetings will be motions to amend the policy structure in some way. Consequently, policy development is not an occasional board chore but its chief occupation."[25]

---

[25] John Carver, *Boards That Make a Difference: A New Design for Leadership in Nonprofit and Public Organizations* (San Francisco: Jossey-Bass, 2006), 72.

SESSION 4:
Leading From a Healthy Governance Model: Creating Clarity and Alignment

> ☑ **HEALTHY GOVERNANCE CHECKLIST**
> CCCA Thriving Boards ◆ Growing Healthy, Effective Boards
>
> **#4. THE BOARD AFFIRMS ITS GOVERNANCE MODEL AND THEOLOGY.**
> ❏ All board members acknowledge their sacred trust as "stewards," not "owners" of the ministry.
> ❏ Board members have a basic understanding of John Carver's "Policy Governance®" model and the four key areas: 1) ends (the taxi), 2) executive limitations (the corral), 3) board-staff linkage, and 4) governing process.
> ❏ Board members agree on where the board is—currently—on the continuum between "policy-making governance" and "hands-on governance"—and where the board wants to be within 12 to 18 months.
> ❏ Board members agree on where their CEO is—currently—on the leadership continuum between "proactive leadership" and "reactive leadership"—and where the board wants the CEO to be within 12 to 18 months.

IN THIS SESSION:

❏ 1. Reflection: Are You a Steward Leader or an Owner Leader?

❏ 2. Worksheet: 10 Board Member Temptations

❏ 3. Quiz: The Continuum Between "Policy-making Governance" and "Hands-on Governance"

❏ 4. Presentation: What's All the Fuss About "Policy Governance®"?

VISIT THE APPENDIX!

What Is Policy Governance®?

Looking for a precise description of the 10 principles of the Policy Governance® model?

Read the official document that lays out what *IS* and *IS NOT* Policy Governance®

1. REFLECTION: ARE YOU A STEWARD LEADER OR AN OWNER LEADER?

Are You a Steward Leader or an Owner-Leader?

"If I could put one Bible verse on the desk of every pastor and every Christian leader in the world, it would be this: 'If we claim to be without sin, we deceive ourselves and the truth is not in us' (1 John 1:8)."

"Perhaps the hardest place to decrease is in the influence and the power we hold over people and decisions. For this reason we find Christian leaders who are overly directive at best and autocratic at worst. As a result we produce churches and ministries that are rife with learned helplessness. By overestimating our worth we help our people depend on us for everything.

"And that dependence feeds into our need to be needed, to be the visionary, to be in control. We tell ourselves that the more we lead in this way, the more our leadership is valued and our presence desired. Of course, this is not real leadership but a counterfeit that contributes to our increase and expands our kingdom. This type of leader is an owner-leader."[26]

NOTES:

---

[26] R. Scott Rodin, *The Steward Leader: Transforming People, Organizations and Communities* (Downers Grove, IL: InterVarsity Press, 2010), 17-19.

❑ 2. WORKSHEET: 10 BOARD MEMBER TEMPTATIONS

What is the GREATEST temptation your board must confront?

☑	CHECK ONE:
	#1. To think and conduct board business under the false assumption that all board members are just like me—and that God has wired us with similar strengths, spiritual gifts and "social styles."
	#2. To assume that all board members are very experienced and effective leaders—just like me—and that we all agree on our board's governance model and that we are in alignment with our CEO's preferred leadership style.
	#3. To confuse the three hats of a board member: governance, volunteer and participant.
	#4. To lower the bar on board member selection—and buy into the ill-informed mantra that just one of the three "W's" are sufficient (Work or Wisdom or Wealth).
	#5. To recruit new board members because of their position versus their passion.
	#6. To rely on my past board and organizational experiences—and rest on my laurels—versus becoming an active life-long learner in board governance best practices. ✓ Etymology for "laurels": based on the literal meaning of laurels (a ring of leaves worn on the head in ancient times as a symbol of victory)
	#7. To assume that all Christ-centered organizations have similar organizational cultures—and to understand one is to understand all.
	#8. To make board decisions based on anecdotes and less-than-stellar analysis—versus requiring thoughtful and objective data, reports and dashboards that are in alignment with a God-inspired mission statement, Big Holy Audacious Goal (B.H.A.G.), crystal clear annual S.M.A.R.T. goals, and a strategic plan rooted in spiritual discernment. (See Drucker quote below.)
	#9. To tilt, perhaps by default, toward one of the three unhealthy board scenarios—and miss the extraordinary opportunity to leverage the "Governance as Leadership" model.[27]
	Add your own temptation! **#10. To** _____

Peter Drucker

"**What everyone knows is usually wrong.**"[28]

---

[27] Richard P. Chait, William P. Ryan, Barbara E. Taylor, *Governance as Leadership: Reframing the Work of Nonprofit Boards* (Hoboken, N.J., John Wiley & Sons, Inc., 2005)

[28] William A. Cohen, *The Practical Drucker: Applying the Wisdom of the World's Greatest Management Thinker* (New York: AMACOM, 2014), 55.

❑ 3. QUIZ: THE CONTINUUM BETWEEN "POLICY-MAKING GOVERNANCE" AND "HANDS-ON GOVERNANCE"

BOARD MEMBER QUIZ Check <u>Column A</u> or <u>Column B</u> to indicate where your board is (in your opinion!):	A POLICY-MAKING ✓	B HANDS-ON ✓
1. Board committees focus ONLY on governance.		
2. Most board members have key volunteer roles.		
3. Board members exclude CEO from input on interviews with future board prospects.		
4. Board meets more than 4 times a year.		
5. "Adjourned is adjourned." Individual board members have no authority outside of board meeting.		
6. All execution and implementation assigned to CEO.		
7. "The board speaks with one voice or not at all."[29]		
8. Board members chair and serve on various operational committees, including Program Committee, Operations Committee, and Fund Development Committee.		
9. Board agenda focuses on short-term problems.[30]		

---

[29] John Carver and Miriam Mayhew Carver, *Carver Guide 1: Basic Principles of Policy Governance* (San Francisco: Jossey-Bass, 1996), 2.
[30] Dan Busby and John Pearson, *More Lessons From the Nonprofit Boardroom: Effectiveness, Excellence, Elephants!* (Winchester, VA: ECFAPress, 2019). (See Lesson 35: "Leverage the 80/20 Rule in the Boardroom.")

Session 4 ◆ Leading From a Healthy Governance Model

WORKSHEET:
Where is your board on the "Policy Governance®" Continuum?
Adapted from John Carver's "Policy Governance®" list of board roles:

☑ **1 THROUGH 10 FOR EACH STATEMENT BELOW:**

"THE STARTER LIST"	ALWAYS...NEVER									
OUR BOARD...	10	9	8	7	6	5	4	3	2	1
1. Sets the board's work plan and agenda for the year and for each meeting.										
2. Determines board training and development needs.										
3. Attends to discipline in board attendance, following bylaws and other self-imposed rules.										
4. Continually improves their expertise as lifelong learners in governance.										
5. Meets with and gathers wisdom from the organization's customers (and "owners").										
6. Establishes the limits of the CEO's authority to budget, administer finances and compensation.										
7. Establishes the results, recipients, and acceptable costs of those results that justify the organization's existence.										
8. Examines monitoring data and determines whether the organization has achieved a reasonable interpretation of board-stated criteria.										
9.										
10.										

John Carver: "**THE PURPOSE OF GOVERNANCE** is to ensure, usually on behalf of others, that an organization achieves what it should achieve while avoiding those behaviors that should be avoided."[31]

---

[31] Carver, *Boards That Make a Difference*, xxvii.

Session 4 ♦ Leading From a Healthy Governance Model

WORKSHEET:

WHERE IS YOUR BOARD ON THIS CONTINUUM?

☑ Check the number that best describes your **board's** operating style today:

High Policy-making………………………………………………High Hands-on

Board Style 10 = High Policy-making 1 = High Hands-on	10	9	8	7	6	5	4	3	2	1

WHERE IS YOUR CEO ON THIS CONTINUUM?

☑ Check the number that best describes your CEO's leadership style today.

Proactive Leadership……………………..…………… Reactive Leadership

CEO Style 10 = Proactive 1 = Reactive	10	9	8	7	6	5	4	3	2	1

What is your analysis of the current styles of your board and CEO?

ANSWER:

Session 4 ◆ Leading From a Healthy Governance Model

WORKSHEET:

WHERE DO YOU WANT YOUR BOARD TO BE IN 12 TO 18 MONTHS?

☑ Check the number that best describes where you want your **board** to be in 12 to 18 months:

High Policy-making………………………………………………High Hands-on

Board Style 10 = High Policy-making 1 = High Hands-on	10	9	8	7	6	5	4	3	2	1

WHERE DO YOU WANT YOUR CEO TO BE IN 12 TO 18 MONTHS?

☑ Check the number that best describes where you want your **CEO** to be in 12 to 18 months:

Proactive Leadership……………………….……………… Reactive Leadership

CEO Style 10 = Proactive 1 = Reactive	10	9	8	7	6	5	4	3	2	1

Discuss where you think the board and CEO are in their current understanding of board and CEO styles—and what are the key steps required to move them to a new position in the next 12 to 18 months (if desired or required)?

ANSWER:

Session 4 ◆ Leading From a Healthy Governance Model

❏ 4. PRESENTATION: WHAT'S ALL THE FUSS ABOUT "POLICY GOVERNANCE®"?

Boards That Make a Difference:
A New Design For Leadership in Nonprofit and Public Organizations
by John Carver

When recruiting new board members, your most experienced recruits will likely ask you about your organization's position on "policy governance®" or the "Carver model" of board governance. There are strong opinions on either side of the policy governance continuum.

➔**For more information:** "The Authoritative Website for the Carver Policy Governance® Model"
www.carvergovernance.com/model.htm

Two Pictures of Policy Governance®

THE TAXI:

THE CORRAL:

WHY POLICY GOVERNANCE®?

HERE'S WHAT GOES WRONG WITH MANY BOARDS: ⬇	➔ SO...INADEQUATE PRESCRIPTIONS ARE DEPLOYED TO SOLVE WHAT GOES WRONG: ⬇
☑ Short-term bias	❏ More involvement
☑ Reactive stance	❏ Less involvement
☑ Reviewing, rehashing, redoing	❏ Board as watchdog
☑ Leaky accountability	❏ Board as cheerleader
☑ Diffuse authority	❏ Board as manager
☑ Complete overload	❏ Board as planner
	❏ Board as adviser
	❏ Board as fundraiser
	❏ Board as communicator

John Carver

"LIKE THE PARENT OF A TWO-YEAR-OLD, the governing board knows it has power but never quite feels truly in charge."[32]

---

[32] Carver, *Boards That Make a Difference*, 257. (See Chapter 10: "Making Meetings Meaningful: Creating the Future More Than Reviewing the Past")

POLICY GOVERNANCE® SUMMARIZED:

4 KEY AREAS	DEFINITIONS[33]
ENDS	"The board defines which human needs are to be met, for whom, and at what cost. Written with a long-term perspective, these mission-related policies embody the board's long-range vision."
EXECUTIVE LIMITATIONS	"The board establishes the boundaries of acceptability within which staff methods and activities can responsibly be left to staff. These limiting policies apply to staff means rather than ends."
BOARD-STAFF LINKAGE	"The board clarifies the manner in which it delegates authority to staff as well as how it evaluates staff performance on provisions of the ends and executive limitation policies."
GOVERNING PROCESS	"The board determines its philosophy, its accountability, and specifics of its own job. The effective design of its own board processes ensures that the board will fulfill its three primary responsibilities: 1. Maintaining links to the ownership 2. Establishing the four categories of written policies 3. Assuring executive performance"

WORKSHEET:

How Will You Address Board Styles When You Recruit New Board Members and a New CEO?
Now that you have studied board models and styles and CEO leadership styles, think about how you will recruit new board members and a new CEO (when that time comes). For example, how will you discern a future board member's preferred style—and address the potential for conflict, if that style doesn't conform to the board's preferred style? How will you discern a CEO candidate's preferred leadership style—and what is that candidate's understanding of Policy Governance®?

ANSWER:

---

[33] Carver, *Boards That Make a Difference*, 37-54. (See Chapter 2: Policy as a Leadership Tool: The Force of Explicit Values)

Session 4 ◆ Leading From a Healthy Governance Model

BONUS RESOURCE
☑ **3 TOOLS FOR CLARIFYING BOARD AND CEO ROLES: PICK 1**

❑ **Option #1: Prime Responsibility Chart**[34]
1-PAGE TEMPLATE

- Reference this one-page chart at every board meeting.
- Eliminate all fuzzy roles!
- Identify a point person (or champion) for every responsibility.
- Change the chart often—because organizations must change often.

HIGHLY RECOMMENDED! ☑ **Option #2: Board Policies Manual (BPM)**
10- TO 15-PAGE TEMPLATE

Good Governance for Nonprofits: Developing Principles and Policies for an Effective Board[35]
by Fredric L. Laughlin and Robert C. Andringa

- Features a 10- to 15-page document with all board policies
- Color commentary on each policy
- Designed to be updated frequently, based on organizational needs and changing internal and external realities
- Simpler and more time-saving option to other approaches
- Although this is not designed as a "faith-based" BPM, the context is built in so you can add the Christ-centered distinctives of your ministry.

❑ **Option #3: The Policy Governance® Model from John Carver**
A MAJOR COMMITMENT TO A VERY PRECISE GOVERNANCE MODEL!

Boards That Make a Difference: A New Design for Leadership in Nonprofit and Public Organizations
by John Carver

- You'll likely need a Carver-trained consultant to help you implement this rigorous policy system.
- Visit: http://www.carvergovernance.com/model.htm
- See a snapshot in the Appendix.

---

[34] Busby and Pearson, *ECFA Tools and Templates for Effective Board Governance* (See the access code for downloading the "Prime Responsibility Chart" template.)
[35] Fredric L. Laughlin and Robert C. Andringa, *Good Governance for Nonprofits: Developing Principles and Policies for an Effective Board* (New York: AMACOM, American Management Association, 2007)

❏ OPTION #1: THE PRIME RESPONSIBILITY CHART

Important! This template is an example only. The details are not prescriptive for every board.

PRIME RESPONSIBILITY CHART[36]
Version 1.0 (Drafted by Carlos, Jennifer and Cameron on Jan. 15, 2019)

P = Prime Responsibility	A = Assistant Responsibility		AP = Approval Required		
BOARD AND STAFF ROLES AND RESPONSIBILITIES	**Board**	**Executive Committee**	**Top Leader (CEO)**	**Exec. VP, or CFO**	**Dept. Heads**
PERSONNEL					
1) Hire and fire the CEO	AP	P			
2) Hire and fire other senior leaders			P		
3) Hire and fire middle management			AP	P	
4) Hire and fire all other staff				AP	P
5) Annual update: employee handbook	AP		AP	P	A
PLANNING					
1) Mission, vision, values	AP		P	A	A
2) Rolling 3-Year Plan Annual Update	AP		P	A	A
3) CEO annual goals	AP	AP	P	A	A
4) Dept. heads annual goals			AP	AP	P
FINANCE					
1) Annual budget	AP	AP	A	P	A
2) Quarterly financial reports	AP			P	
3) Annual audit	AP			P	
4) Non-budgeted expenditures over $___		AP	AP	P	A
Add additional categories, roles, and responsibilities below (as needed)					

IMPORTANT PRINCIPLE! Only one person has "Prime Responsibility" (P). In the absence of a *Board Policies Manual* (see *ECFA Tools and Templates*), this one-page chart is an excellent way to clarify board and staff roles. Update this chart whenever the board edits the policy and label it (for example): Version 3.0 – 4/15/2019.

> "If you don't know what your top three priorities are, you don't have priorities."[37]
>
> "What you measure improves."[38]
>
> Donald Rumsfeld

---

[36] Busby and Pearson, *ECFA Tools and Templates for Effective Board Governance*
[37] Donald Rumsfeld, *Rumsfeld's Rules: Leadership Lessons in Business, Politics, War, and Life* (New York: HarperCollins Publishers, 2013), 304.
[38] Ibid., 85.

SESSION 5

Leveraging the 3 Powerful S's

☑ **S**piritual Gifts
☑ **S**ocial Styles
☑ **S**trengths

SESSION 5:
Leveraging the 3 Powerful S's:
Spiritual Gifts, Social Styles, Strengths

> ☑ **HEALTHY GOVERNANCE CHECKLIST**
> **CCCA Thriving Boards ◆ Growing Healthy, Effective Boards**
>
> **#5. ALL BOARD MEMBERS LEVERAGE THEIR "SWEET SPOTS" WHEN SERVING!**
> ❏ Board members understand board service as a holy calling—and experience joy when serving.
> ❏ The board leverages the spiritual gifts, social styles (or other model), and strengths of each other.
> ❏ Board members are students of the unique strengths and giftedness of their board chair and their CEO.
> ❏ The board chair, CEO and the senior team are students of the strengths and giftedness of all board members.

IN THIS SESSION:

❏ 1. <u>Pop Quiz</u>! Have you ever completed an assessment?

❏ 2. <u>Imagination Moment</u>! What if…every board member was empowered to leverage our unique sweet spots in our holy calling as board members? (The 3 Powerful S's)

❏ 3. <u>Book/Online Assessment</u>. **Spiritual Gifts:** The unique design and "wiring" given by God—*supernaturally*—to every believer so we accomplish His plan for our lives.

❏ 4. <u>Book/Online Assessment</u>. **Clifton StrengthsFinder®:** The 34 themes that describe what we *naturally* do best, per research by Gallup.

❏ 5. <u>Book/Video</u>: **Social Styles:** The easy-to-remember model for understanding our own behavior preferences—and that of others—in how we act, make decisions, and use our time.

Session 5 ◆ Leveraging the 3 Powerful S's

❑ 1. POP QUIZ! HAVE YOU EVER COMPLETED AN ASSESSMENT?

REMAIN STANDING IF...

☑ 1._____

☑ 2._____

☑ 3._____

☑ 4._____

☑ 5._____

WHAT DID YOU OBSERVE IN THE ROOM ABOUT...
- ❑ Myers-Briggs Type Indicator
- ❑ DiSC
- ❑ Enneagram
- ❑ Four Animal Types (Gary Smalley and John Trent)
- ❑ Personality Plus (Florence Littauer)
- ❑ Spirit-Controlled Temperaments (Tim LaHaye)
- ❑ StrengthsFinder
- ❑ Social Styles
- ❑ Birkman Personality Assessment
- ❑ Style of Influence®
- ❑ _____
- ❑ _____

Note: The Greek physician Hippocrates—perhaps—first suggested the four fundamental personality types: sanguine, choleric, melancholic, and phlegmatic. Most formulations include the possibility of mixtures among the types where an individual's personality types overlap and they share two or more temperaments. (Wikipedia)

Frederick Buechner

"The place God calls you to is the place where your deep gladness and the world's deep hunger meet."[39]

---

[39] Frederick Buechner is quoted in *Crafting a Rule of Life: An Invitation to a Well-Ordered Way*, by Stephen A. Macchia (Downers Grove, IL: InterVarsity Press, 2012), 54.

Session 5 ◆ Leveraging the 3 Powerful S's

❑ **2. IMAGINATION MOMENT! What if...every board member was empowered to leverage our unique sweet spots in our holy calling as board members?**

THE 3 POWERFUL S'S

Spiritual Gifts	**BRUCE BUGBEE:** "God has created and designed us with a purpose in mind. We are 'wired' to care about some things more than others. **We have been given spiritual gifts to competently accomplish ministry tasks.** We have also been designed with a personal style of relating to others and the world around us. We have been given a passion."[40] So...knowing all of that, what has God designed you for?
Strengths	**TOM RATH:** "...our studies indicate that people who do have the opportunity to focus on their strengths every day **are six times as likely to be engaged in their jobs** and more than three times as likely to report having an excellent quality of life in general."[41]
Social Styles	**DON GERMAN:** "Interpersonal Versatility is the third dimension to this system. This dimension is a measure of how others view your ability to adapt to different people and situations. **A key principle of understanding social styles is this: There is no good or bad style!**"[42]

---

[40] Bruce Bugbee, *What You Do Best in the Body of Christ: Discover Your Spiritual Gifts, Personal Style, and God-Given Passion*, rev. ed., (Grand Rapids: MI: Zondervan, 2005), 15.
[41] Tom Rath, *StrengthsFinder 2.0* (New York: Gallup Press, 2007), iii.
[42] Don German, "How to Radically Improve Your Communication Skills by Knowing the Preferred 'Social Style' of Your Boss! *Christian Management Report* (October 2005).

Session 5 ◆ Leveraging the 3 Powerful S's

❑ **3. BOOK/ONLINE ASSESSMENT. SPIRITUAL GIFTS:** The unique design and "wiring" given by God—*supernaturally*—to every believer so we accomplish His plan for our lives.

SPIRITUAL GIFTS

❑ **BOOK:** *What You Do Best in the Body of Christ: Discover Your Spiritual Gifts, Personal Style, and God-Given Passion*
by Bruce Bugbee

This is the Spiritual Gifts 101 book. You can also read, of course, Romans 12, Ephesians 4 and many other New Testament chapters.

SPIRITUAL GIFTS LIST

❑ **LIST:** Bruce Bugbee's list of spiritual gifts (from the New Testament):

- ❑ Administration
- ❑ Craftsmanship
- ❑ Creative Communication
- ❑ Encouragement
- ❑ Faith
- ❑ Giving
- ❑ Helps
- ❑ Hospitality
- ❑ Intercession
- ❑ Leadership
- ❑ Mercy
- ❑ Apostleship
- ❑ Prophecy
- ❑ Evangelism
- ❑ Shepherding
- ❑ Teaching
- ❑ Discernment
- ❑ Word of Knowledge
- ❑ Word of Wisdom
- ❑ Healing
- ❑ Interpretation
- ❑ Miracles
- ❑ Tongues

FREE ONLINE SPIRITUAL GIFTS ANALYSIS

The Team Ministry Spiritual Gifts Survey is a discovery tool that provides you with a personalized analysis. Not an exam, but a simple questionnaire giving you a profile of your God-given spiritual gifts.

https://gifts.churchgrowth.org/spiritual-gifts-survey/

☐ **4. BOOK/ONLINE ASSESSMENT. CLIFTON STRENGTHSFINDER®: The 34 themes that describe what we *naturally* do best, per research by Gallup.**

STRENGTHS

Imagine! What if everyone on your board received committee assignments that leveraged their strengths? Each book below includes a unique access code for an online assessment at www.gallupstrengthscenter.com. After you complete the 20- to 30-minute online assessment, you will receive a list (and commentary) of your Top-5 strengths. Many boards compile these strengths into a chart so that committee assignments and volunteer work are delegated according to a person's strengths. Each book includes mini-descriptions of each of the 34 talent themes.

Strengths Based Leadership: *Great Leaders, Teams and Why People Follow*
by Tom Rath and Barry Conchie

According to the Gallup Organization, over 18 million people worldwide have discovered their CliftonStrengths®—their top-five of 34 strengths/talent themes. **Yet...75 percent of the workforce do not leverage their strengths at work every day.** *Yikes!* Instead, many supervisors, bosses and boards focus incorrectly on a leader's weaknesses—instead of his or her strengths. This book also includes four "case studies" of four CEOs from each of the four domains of leadership strength: Executing, Influencing, Relationship Building, and Strategic Thinking.[43]

StrengthsFinder 2.0: *Discover Your CliftonStrengths®*
by Tom Rath

"…our studies indicate that people who do have the opportunity to focus on their strengths every day **are six times as likely** to be engaged in their jobs and more than three times as likely to report having an excellent quality of life in general."[44]

Living Your Strengths: *Discover Your God-Given Talents and Inspire Your Community*
by Albert L. Winseman, Donald O. Clifton, and Curt Liesveld

A BOARD MEMBER: "After serving almost four years on the church board, I had yet to fully know or understand those with whom I was working. The extent of our personal knowledge about one another went little beyond being asked to 'share your favorite movie.' At the initiation of a new church board chair and a new executive pastor, we underwent strengths coaching, both individual and team. Everyone engaged in the process, and I learned more about my teammates in one evening than in all my previous years on the board. It was the most meaningful and significant times we've spent together."[45]

---

[43] Tom Rath and Barry Conchie, *Strengths Based Leadership: Great Leaders, Teams and Why People Follow* (New York: Gallup Press, 2008), 24.
[44] Tom Rath, *StrengthsFinder 2.0* (New York: Gallup Press, 2007), iii.
[45] Albert L. Winseman, Donald O. Clifton, and Curt Liesveld, *Living Your Strengths: Discover Your God-Given Talents and Inspire Your Community, Third Edition* (New York: Gallup Press, 2008), 56.

Session 5 ◆ Leveraging the 3 Powerful S's

☑ STRENGTHS TOOL #1: WALLET-SIZE CARDS[46]

Laminate *and Leverage* Your Strengths!

After your board has completed the CliftonStrengths® assessment, prepare wallet-size laminated cards for each person—as a reminder to "leverage your strengths!"

OPTION 1:

> **JOHN PEARSON ◆ MY TOP-5 STRENGTHS[47]**
>
> 1. **"FOCUS®** - People exceptionally talented in the Focus theme can take a direction, follow through and make the corrections necessary to stay on track. They prioritize, then act."
> 2. **"RESPONSIBILITY®** - People exceptionally talented in the Responsibility theme take psychological ownership of what they say they will do. They are committed to stable values such as honesty and loyalty."
> 3. **"SIGNIFICANCE®** - People exceptionally talented in the Significance theme want to be very important in others' eyes. They are independent and want to be recognized."
> 4. **"BELIEF®** - People exceptionally talented in the Belief theme have certain core values that are unchanging. Out of these values emerges a defined purpose for their lives."
> 5. **"MAXIMIZER®** - People exceptionally talented in the Maximizer theme focus on strengths as a way to stimulate personal and group excellence. They seek to transform something strong into something superb."

OPTION 2:

> **DAN BUSBY ◆ MY TOP-5 STRENGTHS[48]**
>
> LEARNER®
> ACHIEVER®
> CONNECTEDNESS®
> IDEATION®
> BELIEF®
>
> *"I praise you because I am fearfully and wonderfully made; your works are wonderful, I know that full well."*
> Psalm 139:14 (NIV)

MORE RESOURCES:

❑ **Gallup Strengths Center:**
   http://www.gallupstrengthscenter.com

❑ **One-minute YouTube videos of all 34 strengths:**
   www.youtube.com/user/GallupStrengths

---

[46] Busby and Pearson, *ECFA Tools and Templates for Effective Board Governance* (See the access code for downloading selected "Strengths" tools noted on these pages.)
[47] CliftonStrengths® and each of the 34 theme names are trademarks of Gallup, Inc. To discover your top five CliftonStrengths®, please visit the Gallup Strengths Center at https://www.gallupstrengthscenter.com/.
[48] Ibid.

Session 5 ◆ Leveraging the 3 Powerful S's

☑ STRENGTHS TOOL #2: TENT CARDS

Enrich your board and committee meetings with 8.5" x 11" tent cards—highlighting the strengths of each person.

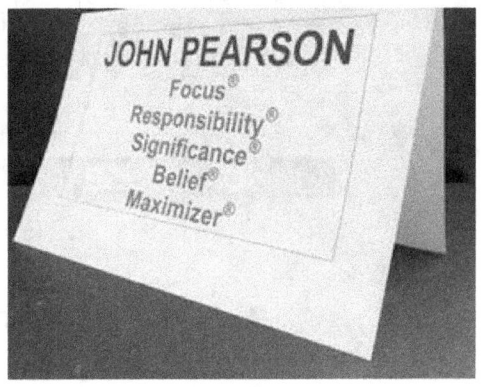

Easy-to-print! Prepare on 8.5" x 11" card stock,
print on BOTH sides, and fold in half.[49]

> "A leader needs to know his strengths as a carpenter knows his tools,
> or as a physician knows the instruments at her disposal.
> What great leaders have in common is that each truly knows his or her
> strengths—and can call on the right strength at the right time. This explains why
> there is no definitive list of characteristics that describes all leaders."[50]
>
> Donald O. Clifton

---

[49] CliftonStrengths® and each of the 34 theme names are trademarks of Gallup, Inc. To discover your top five CliftonStrengths®, please visit the Gallup Strengths Center at https://www.gallupstrengthscenter.com/.
[50] Rath and Conchie, *Strengths Based Leadership*, 13.

Session 5 ◆ Leveraging the 3 Powerful S's

☑ STRENGTHS TOOL #3: CHART

Download the color-coded templates (8.5" x 11" and 11" x 17" landscape version for larger boards).

Our Board's Top-5 Strengths from CliftonStrengths® [51]

NAMES:	Rick	Mike	Cathy	Mark	Maria	
Strength #1						
Strength #2						
Strength #3						
Strength #4						
Strength #5						
EXECUTING						
Achiever®						
Arranger®						
Belief®						
Consistency®						
Deliberative®						
Discipline®						
Focus®						
Responsibility®						
Restorative®						
INFLUENCING						
Activator®						
Command®						
Communication®						
Competition®						
Maximizer®						
Self-Assurance®						
Significance®						
Woo®						
RELATIONSHIP BUILDING						
Adaptability®						
Connectedness®						
Developer®						
Empathy®						
Harmony®						
Includer®						
Individualization®						
Positivity®						
Relator®						
STRATEGIC THINKING						
Analytical®						
Context®						
Futuristic®						
Ideation®						
Input®						
Intellection®						
Learner®						
Strategic®						

Chart Concept: John Pearson

---

[51] CliftonStrengths® and each of the 34 theme names are trademarks of Gallup, Inc. To discover your top five CliftonStrengths®, please visit the Gallup Strengths Center at https://www.gallupstrengthscenter.com/.

OUR BOARD'S TOP-5 STRENGTHS FROM CLIFTONSTRENGTHS® - EXAMPLE[52]

BOARD MEMBERS	RICK BURTON	MIKE PORTER	CATHY JONES	MARK OWENS	MARIA LOPEZ
Strength #1	Belief	Woo	Strategic	Connectedness	Relator
Strength #2	Positivity	Empathy	Maximizer	Woo	Belief
Strength #3	Developer	Positivity	Activator	Belief	Arranger
Strength #4	Connectedness	Communication	Command	Maximizer	Achiever
Strength #5	Strategic	Arranger	Relator	Learner	Focus
EXECUTING					
Achiever®					Achiever
Arranger®		Arranger			Arranger
Belief®	Belief			Belief	Belief
Consistency®					
Deliberative®					
Discipline®					
Focus®					Focus
Responsibility®					
Restorative®					
INFLUENCING					
Activator®			Activator		
Command®			Command		
Communication®		Communication			
Competition®					
Maximizer®			Maximizer	Maximizer	
Self-Assurance®					
Significance®					
Woo®		Woo		Woo	
RELATIONSHIP BUILDING					
Adaptability®					
Connectedness®	Connectedness			Connectedness	
Developer®	Developer				
Empathy®		Empathy			
Harmony®					
Includer®					
Individualization®					
Positivity®	Positivity	Positivity			
Relator®			Relator		Relator
STRATEGIC THINKING					
Analytical®					
Analytical®					
Context®					
Futuristic®					
Ideation®					
Input®					
Intellection®					
Learner®				Learner	
Strategic®	Strategic		Strategic		

Chart Concept: John Pearson

---

[52] CliftonStrengths® and each of the 34 theme names are trademarks of Gallup, Inc. To discover your top five CliftonStrengths®, please visit the Gallup Strengths Center at https://www.gallupstrengthscenter.com/.

☑ STRENGTHS TOOL #4: COFFEE MUGS!

Present a personalized Strengths mug to every board member!

(Photo courtesy of Scott Mackes, Strengths Mugs, www.strengthsmugs.com)

Order at:
www.strengthsmugs.com

←**Recommendation!** Download the Strengths chart template.

Download the 11" x 17" color-coded blank template and add the Top-5 strengths for each board member. The completed template will visually show how "well-rounded" your board is in the four domains of leadership strength (Executing, Influencing, Relationship Building, and Strategic Thinking).[53]

---

[53] The four domains of leadership strength (Executing, Influencing, Relationship Building, and Strategic Thinking) are described in the book, *Strengths Based Leadership: Great Leaders, Teams and Why People Follow*, by Tom Rath and Barry Conchie (New York: Gallup Press, 2008).

Session 5 ◆ Leveraging the 3 Powerful S's

❑ **5. BOOK/VIDEO: SOCIAL STYLES:** The easy-to-remember model for understanding our own behavior preferences—and that of others—in how we act, make decisions, and use our time.

SOCIAL STYLE®

❑ *The Social Styles Handbook: Adapt Your Style to Win Trust,* published by Wilson Learning[54]

Many organizations use the Myers-Briggs Type Indicator, or DISC, or other "personality" type assessments—but few organizations build them thoughtfully into the DNA so CEOs really know their people and their board members (by their styles). The "social styles" system is perhaps the simplest and easiest to remember because the four key words describe the behavior: **Driving, Analytical, Amiable and Expressive.**

❑ *How to Deal With Annoying People: What to Do When You Can't Avoid Them*, by Bob Phillips and Kimberly Alyn[55]

This is the faith-based book on the four social styles, written by Bob Phillips, former executive director of Hume Lake Christian Camps in California. Many board consultants find that 80 percent of most board conflicts are the result of board members not understanding the basic differences between the four social styles.

RESOURCES

❑ Visit Tracom: "The Social Intelligence Company®
https://tracom.com/social-style-training

 ❑ **5-MINUTE VIDEO:**
https://tracom.com/social-style-training/model

❑ Visit The People Bucket:
www.managementbuckets.com/people-bucket

---

[54] Foreword by Larry Wilson, *The Social Styles Handbook: Adapt Your Style to Win Trust,* rev. ed., (USA: Nova Vista Publishing, 2004, 2011).`
[55] Bob Phillips and Kimberly Alyn, *How to Deal With Annoying People: What to Do When You Can't Avoid Them* (Eugene, OR: Harvest House Publishers, 2003/2005).

Session 5 ◆ Leveraging the 3 Powerful S's

SOCIAL STYLES AT-A-GLANCE:

CONTROL
Tasks/Facts
↑

ANALYTICAL Values Thinking ***Avoids** Under Pressure*	**DRIVING** Values Control *Becomes **Autocratic** Under Pressure*
← ASK (*slower-paced*)	TELL (*faster-paced*)→
AMIABLE Values Relationships ***Acquiesces** Under Pressure*	**EXPRESSIVE** Values Intuition ***Attacks** Under Pressure*

↓
EMOTE
Feelings/Intuition

Visit Tracom: "The Social Intelligence Company®
https://tracom.com/social-style-training

6 TIPS ANALYTICAL STYLE

How to Work with Analytical Style People

1. take your **TIME**
2. **COMMUNICATE** clearly & concisely
3. **DON'T PRESSURE** for answers
4. **RESPECT** their processes
5. ask directly for their **FEEDBACK**
6. give them **SPACE**

Courtesy of Tracom: "The Social Intelligence Company®
https://tracom.com/social-style-training

6 TIPS DRIVING STYLE
How to Work with Driving Style People

1. **RESPECT** their time
2. **STICK TO** the facts
3. follow up on your **PROMISES**
4. show your **COMPETENCE**
5. **EARN THEIR TRUST** before expecting it
6. let them have some **CONTROL**

Courtesy of Tracom: "The Social Intelligence Company®
https://tracom.com/social-style-training

6 TIPS AMIABLE STYLE
How to Work with Amiable Style People

1. **APPROACH** conflict carefully
2. **GET TO** know them
3. consider their **PERSPECTIVES**
4. draw out their **OPINIONS**
5. handle issues in **PRIVATE**
6. always be **COURTEOUS**

Courtesy of Tracom: "The Social Intelligence Company®
https://tracom.com/social-style-training

6 TIPS: EXPRESSIVE STYLE

How to Work with Expressive Style People

1. **LAUGH** with them
2. **LISTEN** to their opinions
3. **THINK BIG** picture
4. **RECOGNIZE** their contributions
5. **LIGHTEN UP**
6. **form a FRIENDSHIP**

Courtesy of Tracom: "The Social Intelligence Company®
https://tracom.com/social-style-training

GENERAL OVERVIEW OF THE FOUR SOCIAL STYLES
My Social Style is: _____

Know Your Comfort Zone and <u>Help Others</u> Feel Comfortable
Review this sheet before every board meeting!
Adapted from *Mastering the Management Buckets*, by John Pearson

	ANALYTICALS	**DRIVERS**	**AMIABLES**	**EXPRESSIVES**
Reaction	Slow	Swift	Unhurried	Rapid
Orientation	Thinking and fact	Action and goal	Relationship and peace	Involvement and intuition
Likes	Organization	To be in charge	Close relationships	Much interaction
Dislikes	Involvement	Inaction	Conflict	To be alone
Maximum effort	To organize	To control	To relate	To involve
Minimum concern	For relationships	For caution in relationships	For affecting change	For routine
Behavior directed toward achievement	**PRIMARY EFFORT:** Works carefully and alone	**PRIMARY EFFORT:** Works quickly and alone	SECONDARY EFFORT: Works slowly and with others	SECONDARY EFFORT: Works quickly and with team
Behavior directed toward acceptance	SECONDARY EFFORT: Impress others with precision and knowledge	SECONDARY EFFORT: Impress others with individual effort	**PRIMARY EFFORT:** Gets along as integral member of group	**PRIMARY EFFORT:** Gets along as exciting member of group
Actions	Cautious	Decisive	Slow	Impulsive
Skills	Good problem-solving skills	Good administrative skills	Good counseling skills	Good persuasive skills
Decision-making	Avoids risks, based on facts	Takes risks, based on intuition	Avoids risks, based on opinion	Takes risks, based on hunches
Time frame	Historical	Present	Present	Future
Use of time	Slow, deliberate, disciplined	Swift, efficient, impatient	Slow, calm, undisciplined	Rapid, quick, undisciplined

*Figure 7.6 (Chapter 7, page 121) – Adapted from *The Delicate Art of Dancing With Porcupines* by Bob Phillips (Regal Books). See Note #5 under Core Competency 7: The People Bucket on page 276 of *Mastering the Management Buckets*.[56]

---

[56] John Pearson, *Mastering the Management Buckets*, 121.

Session 5 ◆ Leveraging the 3 Powerful S's

WORKSHEET:
☑ Identify your most STRATEGIC next steps for the 3 Powerful S's:

❏ **Option #1:** Ask board members to take the SF assessment—and create a grid.
❏ **Option #2:** Ask board members to discuss their spiritual gifts at next board meeting.
❏ **Option #3:** Decide which 1, 2 or 3 "Powerful S's" you'll own—and how you'll keep them "top of mind" at every board meeting—and all year.
❏ **Option #4:** Recruit a willing champion who will keep the "3 Powerful S's" on the front burner—especially when new members join your board.
❏ **Option #5:** All of the above!

POINT PERSON	TASK	DEADLINE DATE	DONE DATE

Bruce Bugbee

"Why are you doing what others can do, when you are leaving undone what only you can do?"[57]

---

[57] Bugbee, *What You Do Best in the Body of Christ*, 135 (quoting an unnamed person).

SESSION 6

Keeping the Promise

A Special Presentation

SESSION 6:
Keeping the Promise: *A Special Presentation*

NOTES:

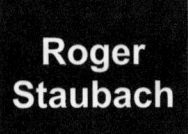
Roger Staubach

"There are no traffic jams along the extra mile."[58]

---

[58] Mac Anderson and Bob Kelly, *The Best of Success: A Treasury of Inspiration* (Naperville, IL: Simple Truths, 2009), 155.

SESSION 7

A Board Prayer

SESSION 7:
A Board Prayer by Dan Bolin

☑ HEALTHY GOVERNANCE CHECKLIST
CCCA Thriving Boards ◆ Growing Healthy, Effective Boards

#7. THE BOARD PRIORITIZES PRAYER AND DISCERNMENT IN EVERY BOARD MEETING.
- ❑ We are clear that we are stewards, not owners, of the ministry—and we prepare agendas with prayer.
- ❑ While we often pray at the beginning and the end of our meetings, we also interject prayers of adoration, confession, thanksgiving, and supplication—throughout our meetings.
- ❑ We are increasingly moving from mere "decision-making" to discernment—as the Holy Spirit guides us.[59]
- ❑ We pray for the "joy of arriving at adjournment closer to one another because we are closer" to our Lord.

IN THIS SESSION:

❑ 1. <u>Praying Together</u>: "A Board Prayer by Dan Bolin"

 "**A BOARD PRAYER**," written by Dan Bolin is featured in *Lessons From the Nonprofit Boardroom* (Second Edition, 2018), by Dan Busby and John Pearson, and *Lessons From the Church Boardroom* (ECFAPress, 2019). This prayer also supplements the materials in the *ECFA Governance Toolbox Series No. 3: Conflicts of Interest - Addressing Board and Organizational Conflicts of Interest: Avoiding Trouble, Trouble, Trouble With Related-Party Transactions*.
www.ECFA.org and ECFA.church

❑ 2. <u>Discerning Together</u>: Moving from Decision-making to Discernment

REFLECT ON...

☑ **THE DISCERNMENT "I.Q." OF BOARD MEMBERS.** "It is also important to involve the right people. One very common leadership mistake is to think that we can take a group of undiscerning individuals and expect them to show up in a leadership setting and all of a sudden become discerning!"[60]

☑ **THE AGENDA. Bathe the agenda in prayer to allow the Holy Spirit to guide board members during the meeting.** "The agenda is the board chair's and CEO's discerning process for aligning with God, His purposes, His will. Spend time in prayer that prepares the entire board for alignment with God and His intentions for the ministry."[61]

☑ _____

---

[59] Ruth Haley Barton, *Pursuing God's Will Together*
[60] Ruth Haley Barton, *Strengthening the Soul of Your Leadership: Seeking God in the Crucible of Ministry, Expanded Edition* (Downers Grove, IL: InterVarsity Press, 2018), 198.
[61] Quoting Ed McDowell in *Lessons From the Nonprofit Boardroom, Second Edition*, by Busby and Pearson (See Lesson 5: "Before the Board Meeting.")

A BOARD PRAYER
Written and Prayed by Dan Bolin
Copyright © 2014 by Dan Bolin Resources, Inc. – dan@danbolin.com
www.refuelinginflight.com

THANK YOU for calling this ministry into existence and for allowing it to serve and care for the people you love.
- ❏ Thank you for the various perspectives represented in this meeting and the things we will learn from one another.
- ❏ Thank you for the privilege of corporately receiving reports, and with one voice establishing policies, discovering direction, setting goals and encouraging those who serve in this ministry.
- ❏ Thank you for the many people whose lives will be influenced through our meeting – other board members, staff, volunteers, donors, participants, vendors, and generations yet unborn who will benefit from the decisions we make today.
- ❏ And God, thank you for entrusting your ministry into our care. Help us to be worthy of the trust that you and others are placing in us.

Father, allow me to **REPORT HONESTLY**.
- ❏ Help me to tell the whole truth not just the parts that make me look good.
- ❏ Let me not bury bad news in mounds of data and detail and don't let me gloss over painful issues or personal failures.
- ❏ Help me to give credit to others and take responsibility for failure and lack of progress.
- ❏ Don't let me trivialize serious issues or magnify minor successes.
- ❏ Let me tell stories and provide statistics that represent accurately.
- ❏ Help me remember that good information provides a smooth pathway to good decisions.

God, as we approach this meeting, help us to **SEE CLEARLY**.
- ❏ Help us to see the issues before us from many perspectives – but ultimately from your perspective. Align our thoughts with your thoughts and our work with your desire.
- ❏ God, help us to see our ministry's strengths and weaknesses and to embrace both.
- ❏ Help us connect the dots between the many good ideas to find the great idea you have for us.
- ❏ Help us to distinguish what is significant from what is superficial,
  what is short-term from what is long-term and
  what is best for me from what is best for all.

Help me to **LISTEN OBJECTIVELY**.
- ❏ Allow me the grace to filter angry words and hear the truth behind what is being said.
- ❏ Help me to listen to the painful heart from which flows harsh comments.

- ❑ Help me to learn from what is legitimate and to discard what is said in spite.
- ❑ Help me to respond to questions with grace and respect.
- ❑ Allow me to focus on what is being said more than how I will respond.

Help me to SPEAK CAUTIOUSLY.
- ❑ Let me use the least words, the least intensity, the least volume needed to be understood.
- ❑ Help me voice my opinions with care, strength and meekness.
- ❑ Help me to ask good questions, open dialogue, explore options, and deepen discussion.
- ❑ Help me to say nothing degrading and nothing that would draw lines of conflict unnecessarily.
- ❑ Help me to affirm and agree whenever possible.
- ❑ Help me to give second voice to a courageous and wise first-voice; those who risk presenting a new, contrary or unrefined perspective.
- ❑ Lord, help me to accept compliments and approval with humility.
- ❑ God, give me the grace to watch with dignity as my proposal fails, and give me humility when my idea meets with approval.

Dear God, give the Board wisdom to PLAN WISELY.
- ❑ Help us to see opportunities and threats and to count the cost and to weigh risks and rewards.
- ❑ Help us to see the possibilities for a better future.
- ❑ Help us to honor the past but give us the courage to abandon the methods that provided yesterday's success but will lead to futility tomorrow.
- ❑ Help us discover and employ the most effective methods to accomplish your mission for this ministry in the days ahead.
- ❑ Help this Board to avoid the herd mentality that could stampede the ministry in a dangerous and reckless direction.
- ❑ Help us to see which decisions are easily reversed and which ones are changed at great peril.

And dear God, help us to REMAIN UNIFIED.
- ❑ Allow every member to express his or her opinion fully.
- ❑ Help us to engage the dreams for the future with harmony and enthusiasm.
- ❑ Help each of us to leave this meeting with the commitment to speak with one voice and to support the group decisions in public and private.
- ❑ Help us to remember that few decisions are worth the divisions caused by dominant winning or belligerent losing.
- ❑ Help us to seek your glory and not ours.
- ❑ Grant us the joy of arriving at adjournment closer to one another because we are closer to you.

Amen

SESSION 8

The Board's Role in Embracing the Donor

Part 1: The 3 R's
- ☑ **R**elationship
- ☑ **R**esource
- ☑ **R**omance

SESSION 8:
The Board's Role in Embracing the Donor
Part 1: The 3 R's (Relationship, Resource, Romance)[62]

> **☑ HEALTHY GOVERNANCE CHECKLIST**
> **CCCA Thriving Boards ◆ Growing Healthy, Effective Boards**
>
> **#8. BOARD MEMBERS AFFIRM THEIR IMPORTANT ROLES WITH DONORS.**
> ❑ Board member recruitment and orientation includes expectations about generous giving.
> ❑ Board member recruitment and orientation includes affirmations about building relationships with others.
> ❑ Board members are coached and each board member's development role is customized according to a board member's 3 Powerful S's (Spiritual Gifts, Strengths, and Social Styles—see Session 5).
> ❑ Board members affirm and live out the ministry's written "Theology of Development."[63]

IN THIS SESSION:

❑ 1. <u>RELATIONSHIP</u>: Development is all about relationship.

❑ 2. <u>RESOURCE</u>: Definition of a donor.

❑ 3. <u>ROMANCE</u>: Setting the stage for romance.

---

[62] Content in this session is copyrighted by Nancy L. Nelson, © 2019. All rights reserved.
[63] Frank and Rodin, *Development 101*, 7-17. (See also "An Example of a Theology of Development" on pages 143-148.)

Session 8 ◆ The Board's Role in Embracing the Donor: (Part 1)

THE 3 R's:

RELATIONSHIP

❑ **1. DEVELOPMENT IS ALL ABOUT RELATIONSHIP**
- We are all hardwired to be in relationship.
- We are all hardwired to be involved in something bigger than ourselves.

RESOURCE

❑ **2. DEFINITION OF A DONOR**
Someone who gives a **resource**. It can be:
- Prayer
- Volunteer time, expertise
- "Gift-in-Kind" (GIK) like hay for horses
- Money
- A future gift written into their estate plan

ROMANCE

❑ **3. SETTING THE STAGE FOR THE ROMANCE**
The Essentials of Development
- Prayer
- Case Statement
- Development Plan
- Segmented Donor List
- Development Team

Nancy Nelson

"**At the deepest level people want to be involved in something bigger than themselves.** They crave relationships and meaning in life. God has hard-wired us this way. Don't make development into a transaction, don't just center on the 'ask.' Attend to it as a romance, a relationship that ends up being transformational."[64]

---

[64] Nancy L. Nelson, *Embracing the Donor: Stories From the Trenches* (from the forthcoming book).

EMBRACE OF THE DONOR
© 2019 Nancy L. Nelson. All rights reserved.

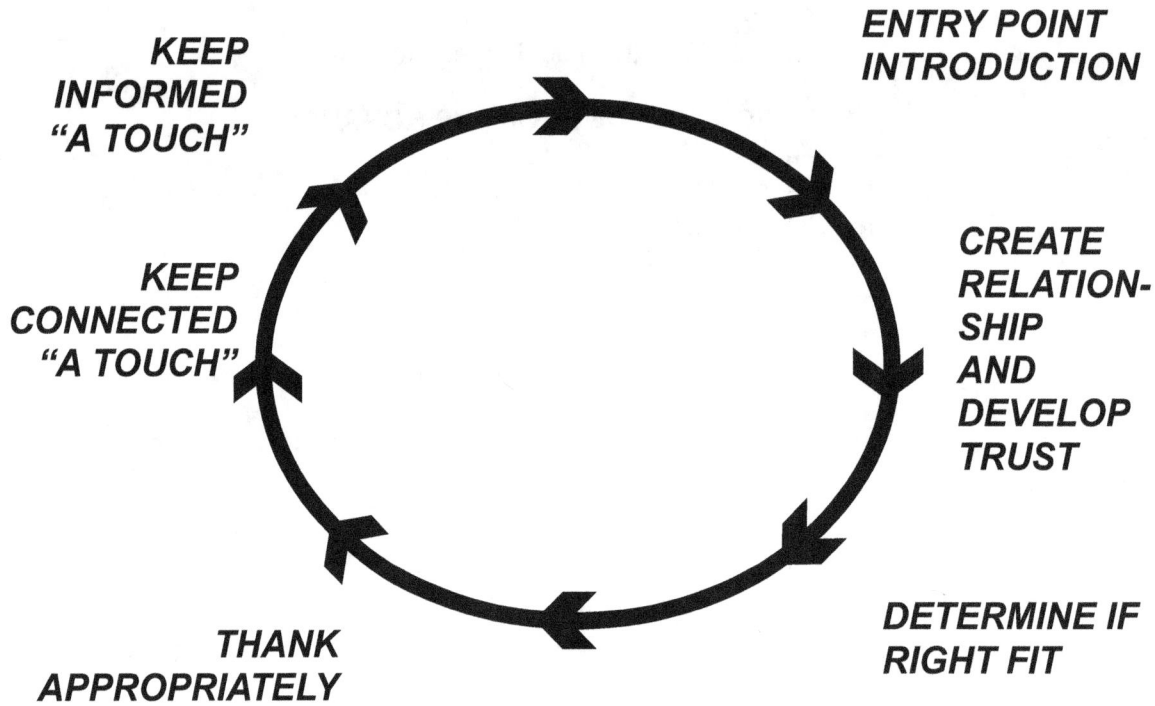

Session 8 ◆ The Board's Role in Embracing the Donor: (Part 1)

LET THE ROMANCE BEGIN!

1. **Introduction: The Entry Point Into the Embrace**
   - A participant (or a relative) in your camp, or someone who has benefited from your camp in some way
   - Introduction from a board member or someone involved with your camp
   - Come to a fund-raising event or an awareness-raising event.
   - Someone with common goals/interests

2. **Start developing relationship and trust**
   - Be honest, be who you are, ALWAYS.
   - It's not only about your camp, it's also about the prospective donor as well.
   - Be there, engage in things that interest them.
   - Do what you say you will do.

3. **Determine if it's a good fit**
   - Suggest a tour.
   - Find out about them….LISTEN to their story.
   - If not the right fit, direct them to another organization that's a better fit for where their passion is.

4. **Make the "ask"**
   - At the right time, when you are pretty confident of a "YES"
   - For the right resource….time, expertise, money, GIK, and/or prayer
   - For the right amount…usually requires starting small until there's time to develop more trust and exposure

5. **Thank appropriately**
   - Thank them ASAP.
   - Know your donor, thank them how they want to be thanked.
   - See "35 Ways to Say Thank You or Do Donor Touches"

6. **Keep them connected and informed**
   - Give 2 or 3 "touches" that convey you are interested in them as individuals as well.
   - Let them know the "inside-information" of what's happening at camp.
   - Tell stories that connect them to the purpose of your camp.
   - Share with them the impact of their giving.

7. **Keep the romance alive and hot**
   - Do the embrace over and over again, getting tighter all the time.
   - Let them feel the camp's passion and know that their contribution helps fuel the passion.
   - Invite them to be on the inside: staff devotions, staff retreat, special planning meetings, etc.
   - Keep hugging them back.
   - Watch for the sparks that continue to turn the resource engine.

8. **Keep the mystery in the romance**
    - Remember the Mars and Venus differences….some will want more facts; others will want more relationship.
    - Remember the importance of trust in relationships: don't do ANYTHING that breaks trust.

9. **Integrate fully for the long haul**
    - Listen for when they begin using the personal pronoun "we" when referring to your camp.
    - Listen for when your camp becomes part of their story, and they carry your camp close to their heart.
    - Watch for the joy when the donor is pulled so close they feel the heartbeat of God in the Kingdom work and their hearts are transformed in the process.

Session 8 ◆ The Board's Role in Embracing the Donor: (Part 1)

35 WAYS TO SAY THANK YOU OR DO "DONOR TOUCHES"

Nancy Nelson

"The six most important words in development are: **THANK YOU, THANK YOU, THANK YOU!**

Saying thank you and appreciating someone is one of the foundational pieces of relationship building. Not all donors are alike. Find the way they like to be thanked. Make gratitude a way of life."[65]

1. Send receipt letter with special personal note.

2. Send something meaningful with their receipt (examples: newspaper clipping with grandkid in it, article on empty-nesting, grieving, etc.).

3. Hand-deliver the receipt and say thank you in person.
    - When and where most convenient for them
    - Listen deeply to them, get them to talk, to tell their story.
    - If it is a reoccurring gift, get creative in delivering receipt.

4. Send "Thank You" note card, hand-written.

5. Immediate phone call, TEXT message, or FACEBOOK private message: "Wow, we just opened the mail, thank you for your gift! I'm ready to dance on my desk!"

6. The "Email Cup of Coffee" (*means*: "Grab a cup of coffee and read my long personal email.")

7. Deliver a small thank you gift to them.
    - Hot cinnamon rolls, home-made bread, or a plate of cookies from the camp kitchen
    - A small valentine candies on Valentine's Day with note, "Thanks for keeping Camp close to your heart!"
    - Christmas gift of notecards with camp scenes or homemade granola from the camp kitchen
    - A picture with them in it taken at Camp or at a fund-raising event

8. Take them on a tour.
    - If possible get them on your camp's turf.
    - If that isn't possible, bring the tour to them via a DVD.

9. Share a favorite book with them or read one of their favorite books, especially one they have authored like their family's history.

10. "Partners-In-Ministry" Appreciation Event

11. Feature them in an article for your newsletter or at an event to help tell the camp's story.

12. Attend significant family events in a donor's life (retirement, wedding, memorials, etc.).

---

[65] Nancy L. Nelson, *Embracing the Donor: Stories From the Trenches* (from the forthcoming book).

13. Hang out with someone important to them on their behalf.

14. Invite to special staff events, like devotions, all-day staff meetings or staff retreat.

15. "Thank you" lunches or dinners held at a staff member's home

16. Connect them to others (connecting the dots!).

17. Invite to a dedication service all who have helped make something possible.

18. Have a plaque hung in honor or memory of someone.

19. Present a surprise "thank you" to a volunteer in public.

20. Recognize with an extra-special meaningful gift.

21. Help another non-profit on a donor's behalf.

22. Accompany them to an event that they don't want to go to alone.

23. Accept speaking engagements that donors ask for (for their church, school, etc.).

24. Telephone "Thank-a-thon" to donors by staff and board of directors

25. Bring them to Rotary, Kiwanis, Lion's Club, or Chamber of Commerce to introduce them as your friend and friend of your camp.

26. Special "thank you" bags stuffed with goodies for the board of directors

27. Christmas banquet for board of directors (they are volunteers too!)

28. Board retreat for board members/spouses

29. Special time of thanks for board members going off the board complete with a picture frame loaded with digital pictures of things they helped to make happen.

30. Weave donor "thank you's" into other events going on in the life of the camp. Invite to closing session of kids camps, etc.—places you need to be at anyway.

31. Accept invitations to stuff that matters to them, even if they can't be there themselves.

32. Cater a meal to them or bring flowers when they are sick.

33. Give them direct access to you via your cell phone.

34. Hug them.

35. Pray for them.

Session 8 ◆ The Board's Role in Embracing the Donor: (Part 1)

9 GROUP DISCUSSION QUESTIONS

DISCUSS AND CHECK YOUR RESPONSE:

❑ **#1. SETTING THE STAGE.** Have you set the stage for the relationship, the backdrop for the romance?
On a scale of 1-5, rate the following:

SETTING THE STAGE FOR THE RELATIONSHIP	NON-EXISTENT (1)...............FULLY/EXCELLENTLY IN PLACE (5)				
Prayer	1	2	3	4	5
Case Statement	1	2	3	4	5
Development Plan	1	2	3	4	5
Segmented Donor List	1	2	3	4	5
Development Team	1	2	3	4	5

❑ **#2. STRENGTHS.** Have your key people completed the CliftonStrengths® assessment?
https://www.gallupstrengthscenter.com/

☑ CHECK:	YES	NO	WILL DO ASAP!
Board Members			
Executive Director			
Development Staff			

❑ **#3. STRATEGIC PLAN.** Does your camp have a strategic plan in place so you know what you are raising resources for?
  ❑ Yes
  ❑ No

❑ **#4. YOUR INVOLVEMENT.** Where do you see yourself being involved in the "Embrace of the Donor?"
Check one or more:
  ❑ Helping get one or more of the essentials of development in place:
    #1. Prayer
    #2. Case Statement
    #3. Development Plan
    #4. Segmented Donor List
    #5. Development Team

  ❑ Introducing people to Camp
    #1. Inviting to participate in one of your programmed camps
    #2. Inviting to a fund-raising or awareness-raising event
    #3. Opening up your network, arranging an introductory meeting

  ❑ Developing trust/determining the fit

Session 8 ◆ The Board's Role in Embracing the Donor: (Part 1)

❑ Being involved in "asking" for the gift
  #1. Going along with the Executive Director or Development Director on a visit
  #2. Actually doing the presentation, including "the ask."

❑ Thanking the donors

❑ Doing on-going "touches" to keep the donors connected with the mission/results

❑ **#5. TRAINING.** Circle the number below that best describes whether or not your camp has training in place to prepare board members for participating in raising resources.

NON-EXISTENT (1)...............FULLY/EXCELLENTLY IN PLACE (5)				
1	2	3	4	5

❑ **#6. DEFINED EXPECTATIONS.** Circle the number below that best describes whether or not your camp has defined expectations for the board's role in raising resources, starting with the interview process before coming on the board.

NON-EXISTENT (1)...............FULLY/EXCELLENTLY BEING DONE (5)				
1	2	3	4	5

❑ **#7. SETTING THE EXAMPLE.** Circle the number below that best describes whether or not all board members are setting the example in giving of their resources, including money.

NO BOARD MEMBERS (1)...............ALL BOARD MEMBERS (5)				
1	2	3	4	5

❑ **#8. ROLE OF THE BOARD.** Read Chapter 3, "The Role of the Board in Development" in *Development 101* by John Frank and R. Scott Rodin (you will receive this book in the spring session).[66]

❑ **#9. PRAYER.** Are you willing to pray this prayer, based on Matthew 11:29-30?

A Prayer by Nancy Nelson

"Abba, embrace me. Pull me so close. Let me feel your heart beat. Holy Spirit, let me smell your breath. I want to walk with you, work with you, and watch how YOU do it. Jesus, teach me the unforced rhythms of grace. In your Name, Jesus, I pray, for YOUR Kingdom purposes to be accomplished."[67]

BASED ON MATTHEW 11:29-30, *THE MESSAGE*

---

[66] Frank and Rodin, *Development 101*, 27-42.
[67] Adapted from *Stories of Sheer Pure Grace*, by Nancy L. Nelson (Stanwood, WA: Warm Beach Camp and Conference Center, 2017), 103.

Session 8 ♦ The Board's Role in Embracing the Donor: (Part 1)

 Visit the Appendix for **More Resources** for the Board's Role In Embracing the Donor

SESSION 9

Strategic Planning

Does Your Board Own the Strategy?

SESSION 9:
Strategic Planning:
Does Your Board Own the Strategy?

> ☑ **HEALTHY GOVERNANCE CHECKLIST**
> CCCA Thriving Boards ◆ Growing Healthy, Effective Boards
>
> **#9. THE BOARD AFFIRMS THE STRATEGIC PLAN AND OWNS THE STRATEGY.**
> ❑ The board ensures that a robust strategic planning process is built into the organization's DNA—year-round.
> ❑ The staff creates the strategic plan—with significant counsel from the board—and the board approves the plan.
> ❑ The strategic plan is forward-looking and visionary, and is graphically visualized with tools such as "The Rolling 3-Year Strategic Plan" (a one-page summary) and a Big HOLY Audacious Goal (BHAG).
> ❑ A two-page strategy document is available at every board meeting—and the board OWNS the strategy.

IN THIS SESSION:

❑ 1. QUIZ: The 14 Questions Every Board Member Must Ask

❑ 2. KEY QUESTION: Does Your Board Own the Strategy?

❑ 3. THE STRATEGIC PLAN: The 7 Reasons Why Strategic Plans Fail

❑ 4. THE STRATEGIC PLAN: One Planning Approach

❑ 5. HOMEWORK! Making Strategic Decisions to Ensure Sustainability

---

Eugene Fram and Jerry Talley

"**STRATEGIC PLANS ARE MOST VULNERABLE** not in their development, but in their implementation. And implementation often hinges on some measurable indication of progress. Without those metrics, the plan is a group of intentions always on the verge of greatness. Without hard data on which to anchor organizational outcomes, the organization can wobble off course without a clear warning signal."[68]

Abstract of the article:

"Without some way of measuring their impact on the community, nonprofit boards can easily fall back into monitoring staff activities, mistaking efforts for outcomes. But developing useful metrics can be a painful, costly, and distracting process. Rather than demanding statistical rigor, the authors argue that even imperfect metrics can be used well in a process that leads to genuine organizational improvements."

---

[68] Jerry L. Talley and Eugene H. Fram, "Using Imperfect Metrics Well: Tracking Progress and Driving Change," *Leader to Leader*, Winter 2010, 52-58.

Session 9 ◆ Strategic Planning: Does Your Board Own the Strategy?

❑ 1. QUIZ: THE 14 QUESTIONS EVERY BOARD MEMBER MUST ASK

Owning Up:
The 14 Questions
Every Board Member Needs to Ask[69]
by Ram Charan

☑ **CIRCLE: YES, MAYBE, OR NO…FOR THESE 14 CRITICAL AREAS:**

5 = Absolutely Yes!
4 = Pretty Much Yes
3 = Maybe or Not Sure
2 = Probably No
1 = Definitely No!

No.	Adapted from *Owning Up*	Your Score
1	Our board composition is right for the challenge ahead. (board recruitment)	5 4 3 2 1
2	We are addressing the risks that could send our camp over the cliff. (risk management)	5 4 3 2 1
3	We are prepared to do our job well when a crisis erupts. (crisis management)	5 4 3 2 1
4	We are well prepared to name our next CEO/Executive Director. (succession planning)	5 4 3 2 1
5	**Our board really does own the camp's strategy. (strategic planning)**	5 4 3 2 1
6	We know how to get the information we need to govern well. (metrics and information flow)	5 4 3 2 1
7	Our CEO/Executive Director compensation is at the right level. (executive compensation/benefits)	5 4 3 2 1
8	We have reviewed the concept of "a lead director." (for nonprofits: perhaps an enhanced role for the board chair role)	5 4 3 2 1
9	Our governance committee is best of breed. (understanding policy governance)	5 4 3 2 1
10	We know how to get the most value out of our limited time. (board meetings/board work)	5 4 3 2 1
11	Our executive sessions help the board own up to our responsibilities. (executive sessions)	5 4 3 2 1
12	Our board's self-evaluation process improves our functioning and our output. (board self-assessment)	5 4 3 2 1
13	We prohibit board members from micromanaging. (the 3 hats: governance, volunteer, participant)	5 4 3 2 1
14	We are prepared to work with activist shareholders and their proxies. (for nonprofits: we know what our supporting customers value)	5 4 3 2 1

---

[69] Ram Charan, *Owning Up*

❏ 2. KEY QUESTION: DOES YOUR BOARD OWN THE STRATEGY?

"There is nothing more important for a CEO…
→ than having the right strategy and right choice of goals.

And for the board…
→ the right strategy is second only to having the right CEO."[70]

4 QUESTIONS:

❏ 1. What is strategy?

"…strategy is a singular thing; there is one strategy for a given business—not a set of strategies. It is one integrated set of choices:
- what is our winning aspiration;
- where will we play;
- how will we win;
- what capabilities need to be in place;
- and what management systems must be instituted?"[71]

❏ 2. Why is strategy important?

❏ 3. What is strategy's relationship to the strategic plan?

❏ 4. What is your camp's strategy?

---

[70] Ram Charan, *Owning Up*, 68.
[71] Roger Martin, "Don't Let Strategy Become Planning," *HBR Blog Network*, Feb. 5, 2013, https://hbr.org/2013/02/dont-let-strategy-become-plann.

Session 9 ◆ Strategic Planning: Does Your Board Own the Strategy?

❑ 3. THE STRATEGIC PLAN: THE 7 REASONS WHY STRATEGIC PLANS FAIL[72]

☑ **Check the box that might be your most challenging issue:**

❑ **1. Event Thinking**
Strategic planning is viewed as an event or a task, instead of a transformational ongoing process.

❑ **2. Top-Down Ego**
Strategic planning is created top-down and characterized by ego and arrogance, instead of humility and listening.

❑ **3. Interruption**
Strategic planning is seen as an "add-on" interruption to my "real work," instead of becoming absolutely core to my role.

❑ **4. Extra Expense**
Strategic planning is allocated as an extra expense (that is often cut) instead of a critical core investment.

❑ **5. Binder Syndrome**
Strategic planning conjures up complex and time-consuming exercises and 3-ring binders, instead of being the servant to a simple and elegant plan that is grounded in the alignment between the mission, BHAG, and S.M.A.R.T. goals.

❑ **6. Sacred Cows**
Strategic planning "economizes" by involving fewer and "safer" stakeholders who honor tradition, dead horses and sacred cows, versus out-of-the-box dangerous ideas!

❑ **7. Pseudo Prayer**
Strategic planning, for the Christ-follower, gives only a wink and a prayer to holy input, versus an extraordinary process of assembling spiritually discerning people together to hear from God—who then joyfully follow His plan.

BONUS REASON!
❑ **8. Verbal Fuzz**
Strategic planning festers in a "verbal draft" purgatory, versus becoming a disciplined process that is both written and implemented.

"I learned to write to burn the fuzz off my thinking."[73]

---

[72] Busby and Pearson, *ECFA Tools and Templates for Effective Board Governance* (Adapted from the tool, "The Rolling 3-Year Strategic Plan Placemat" – See instructions for assessing the board's readiness for planning.)
[73] Fred Smith, Sr., *Breakfast With Fred,* (Ventura, CA: Regal Books, 2007), 138.

Session 9 ◆ Strategic Planning: Does Your Board Own the Strategy?

❑ 4. THE STRATEGIC PLAN: ONE PLANNING APPROACH[74]
A Strategic Plan Task Force (Small Teams with Big Tasks!)

Here is one planning model to consider. Use this 3-ring binder table of contents to create **"The Rolling 3-Year Strategic Plan Process and Schedule."** This worksheet lists the chronological steps a task force might follow when creating the strategic plan. Small teams will address niche assignments and then share critical information and findings with the task force, culminating in the one-page Strategic Plan Placemat. Read *ECFA Tools and Templates for Effective Board Governance* for commentary on the small teams and their big tasks!

ABC Organization's Rolling 3-Year Strategic Plan Process and Schedule[75]
GOAL: Final Draft (Version 4.0) to Board: Sept. 15, 2019 Deadline
Updated by: Emelia Anderson on March 1, 2019

3-RING BINDER TABLE OF CONTENTS (15 tabs)

TAB	Strategic Plan Tasks and Teams (generally completed in this chronological order)	Champion* *Appointed on 12/15/18	1st Draft Deadline
12	**Planning to Plan: Readiness Assessment** The 7 Reasons Why Strategic Plans Fail	Facilitator	
12	**The 5 Most Important Questions You Will Ever Ask About Your Organization** (Jan. 8 session)	Facilitator	
4	Mission, Vision, Values, BHAG		
5	Our Customers and What They Value		
6A	Environmental Scan		
6B	S.W.O.T. Analysis		
6C	Trends (and Trendspotting Exercise)		
6D	Assumptions ("The Radar Report")		
7	Spiritual Discernment Process (ongoing: beginning to end)		
8	Three-Year Visionary Priorities (by department)		
9	Top-5 Goals for Year One		
10	Board and Senior Team S.M.A.R.T. Goals and Monthly Dashboard Reports		
11	Communicating Our Results (4 Creative Options)		
12	Appendix		
1	Introduction		
2	Organization-at-a-Glance and Historical Snapshot		
3A	Executive Summary		
3B	The Rolling 3-Year Strategic Plan Placemat		
	SUPPLEMENTARY RESOURCES:		
13	Customized Strategic Plan Versions (Board, Staff, Volunteers, Donors, etc.)		
14	*HOOPLA!* Celebration		
15	Update of Annual Planning Calendar		

---

[74] Busby and Pearson, *ECFA Tools and Templates for Effective Board Governance* (Adapted from the tool, "The Rolling 3-Year Strategic Plan Placemat" – See book for commentary on each of the 15 sections of the binder.)
[75] Adapted from John Pearson's three-day workshop, "The Rolling 3-Year Strategic Plan Workshop: Build It. Execute It. Update It. Year After Year!" http://managementbuckets.com/workshops

Session 9 ◆ Strategic Planning: Does Your Board Own the Strategy?

5 ELEMENTS

☐ 1. The Process	Select a facilitator/consultant that has a track record for scaling Mt. Everest—and empower that person to select the methodology that has worked well for him or her in the past.
☐ 2. The People	Board/staff task force? Staff-only task force with regular updates to the board? Either way, leverage their CliftonStrengths.®
☐ 3. The Placemat	Wordsmith the one-page placemat with prayerful discernment and an eye to communicating the plan to multiple customers (board, staff, donors, clients, volunteers, etc.).
☐ 4. The Proclamation	Get the plan off the shelf and into the streets! Completing the plan is just the start. Now you must sell the plan.
☐ 5. The Progress	Monitor Results: Dashboards. Targets. Measurements. Metrics. Monthly Updates. *Make strategic planning an on-going, year-round process—not a one-time event.*

7 STEPS

☐ **Step 1: Appoint a Task Force**—generally a combination of key staff and two or three board members.
☐ **Step 2: Create the Planning Calendar**—for most organizations without a written strategic plan, this process might range from three to nine months.
☐ **Step 3: Seek buy-in**—ensure that the CEO (or senior pastor), senior team, and the board agree that the time is right for a strategic planning process and that there is passion, time, and budget to accomplish the plan. (*You never have a second chance to make a first impression.*)
☐ **Step 4: Appoint or retain a Facilitator or Consultant**—discern if you have internal expertise to facilitate this process or if you need to recruit a volunteer or retain a consultant.
☐ **Step 5: Appoint "Champions"** for each section of the plan (Tabs 1 to 15). If this is your first plan, the CEO may prefer to be the champion for Tab 4: Mission, Vision, Values, BHAG.
☐ **Step 6: Plan a *HOOPLA!* Celebration**—create the expectation that you will be successful and put a celebration date on the calendar and assign your best party-planner to organize the event.[76]
☐ **Step 7: Affirm the Annual Planning Calendar**—to ensure that this is a "rolling" three-year plan (that adds one more year every year—so you are always looking ahead three years), set key target dates for the next 12 months. Build strategic planning into the DNA of your organization so it's similar to your budgeting and monthly financial reporting cycle—*not a one-time annual event that provokes groans and excuses!*

View how the ProService team celebrated their achievement of a major quarterly goal, as noted in *Scaling Up*. Search "Happy ProService" on YouTube.[77]

---

[76] Read Chapter 10, "The Hoopla! Bucket" in *Mastering the Management Buckets*, by John Pearson (Ventura, CA: Regal Books, 2008).
[77] Read more about ProService and quarterly themes and celebrations/rewards in *Scaling Up*, by Verne Harnis, 153-159.

Session 9 ◆ Strategic Planning: Does Your Board Own the Strategy?

❑ 5. HOMEWORK! MAKING STRATEGIC DECISIONS TO ENSURE SUSTAINABILITY

Is "nonprofit sustainability" an oxymoron or a critical plank in your accountability/transparency process with donors and staff?

Nonprofit Sustainability:
Making Strategic Decisions for Financial Viability[78]
by Jeanne Bell, Jan Masaoka and Steve Zimmerman

❑ **HOMEWORK #1:** Assemble your staff and/or board and draw the Dual Bottom Line Matrix Map on your flipchart or whiteboard—and then plot every program, service, and product you provide—into one of the appropriate four quadrants. (See next page.)

High Mission Impact Low Sustainability ♥	High Mission Impact High Sustainability ★
Low Mission Impact Low Sustainability 🛑	Low Mission Impact High Sustainability 🌳

"The Dual Bottom Line" matrix map addresses mission impact and financial sustainability—with four easy-to-remember icons:

    Hearts: High Mission Impact, Low Profitability/Sustainability
    Stars: High Mission Impact, High Profitability/Sustainability

    Stop Sign: Low Mission Impact, Low Profitability/Sustainability
    Money Tree: Low Mission Impact, High Profitability/Sustainability

---

[78] Jeanne Bell, Jan Masaoka and Steve Zimmerman, *Nonprofit Sustainability: Making Strategic Decisions for Financial Viability* (San Francisco: Jossey-Bass, 2010), 25.

Session 9 ◆ Strategic Planning: Does Your Board Own the Strategy?

HOMEWORK #1: Assemble your staff and/or board and draw the Dual Bottom Line Matrix Map on your flipchart or whiteboard—and then plot every program, service, and product you provide—into one of the appropriate four quadrants. (Bring your "Top-10" list to the Spring Session.)

Our Top-10 Programs, Products and Services
Business/Ministry Model Worksheet: In Pursuit of Sustainability!

High Mission Impact Low Sustainability	High Mission Impact High Sustainability
♥	★
Low Mission Impact **Low Sustainability**	**Low Mission Impact** **High Sustainability**
🛑	🌳

Session 9 ◆ Strategic Planning: Does Your Board Own the Strategy?

❏ **HOMEWORK #2:** If you volunteered to bring a "15-MINUTE OVERVIEW" of a chapter from *Scaling Up*, please do a rehearsal at a board meeting first—and then present your overview at the Spring Session. In your presentation, note your "three takeaway 'bumper sticker'" points:[79]

#1. The big idea for our staff is: _____.
#2. The big idea for our board is: _____.
#3. I'm guessing that your biggest question about this chapter is: "_____."

Format: 7 minutes of presentation + 8 minutes for Q&A = 15 minutes

SCALING UP:
How a Few Companies Make It...and Why the Rest Don't
Mastering the Rockefeller Habits 2.0[80]
by Verne Harnish

15 Minutes Including Q&A:
A Plan to Save the World From Lousy Presentations
by Joey Asher

No.	CHAPTER TITLE	ASSIGNED TO:
INTRODUCTION		
1	THE OVERVIEW: People, Strategy, Execution, Cash	
2	THE BARRIERS: Leadership, Infrastructure, and Marketing	
SCALING UP: PEOPLE		
3	THE LEADERS: The FACe and PACe of the Company	
4	THE TEAM: Attracting and Hiring	
5	THE MANAGERS (COACHES): Keeping and Growing (Educating) the Team	
SCALING UP: STRATEGY		
6	THE CORE: Values, Purpose, and Competencies	
7	THE 7 STRATA OF STRATEGY: The Framework for Dominating Your Industry	
8	THE ONE-PAGE STRATEGIC PLAN: The Tool for Strategic Planning	
SCALING UP: EXECUTION		
9	THE PRIORITY: Focus, Finish Lines, and Fun	
10	THE DATA: Powering Prediction	
11	THE MEETING RHYTHM: The Heartbeat of the Organization	
SCALING UP: CASH		
12	THE CASH: Accelerating Cash Flow	
13	THE ACCOUNTING: Driving Profitability	
14	THE POWER OF ONE: 7 Key Financial Levers	

---

[79] Joey Asher, *15 Minutes Including Q&A: A Plan to Save the World From Lousy Presentations* (Atlanta, GA: Persuasive Speaker Press, 2010), 10.
[80] Verne Harnish, *Scaling Up*

Session 9 ◆ Strategic Planning: Does Your Board Own the Strategy?

❏ HOMEWORK #3: Review the following sessions in this workbook BEFORE the Spring Session and come prepared to share your insights:

Session	Worksheet Title	Page	☑ Staff Assignment	☑ Board Assignment

The Big Idea from Jim Collin's Latest Monograph:
TURNING THE FLYWHEEL[81]

"To maximize the flywheel you need to understand how your specific flywheel turns."

Collins illustrates the uniqueness of the flywheel approach with flywheel diagrams from seven companies and nonprofits, including Ware Elementary School, located on the Fort Riley army base in Kansas. Deb Gustafson, the principal, first read the *Good to Great and the Social Sectors* monograph and was absolutely giddy! "When I got to the part about turning the flywheel, I was bouncing up and down out of my seat," she said.

And note this: Jeff Bezos "…considered Amazon's application of the flywheel concept 'the secret sauce.'" But this caution: you need to understand how your organization's specific flywheel turns—and the sequence of the components. **Collins notes seven key steps for capturing your unique flywheel approach—plus this warning: don't feature more than four to six components.**

He includes flywheel diagrams from Amazon, Vanguard, Intel, Giro, Ware Elementary School, Ojai Music Festival, and the Cleveland Clinic. (Wow—Collins must have a love affair with Cleveland. In his first monograph, he highlights "Greatness at the Cleveland Orchestra"—one of my favorite examples for nonprofits.)

He packs all of this—and more—into just 29 pages, plus the appendix. But this is all you're getting in this review; otherwise you wouldn't need to buy the book.

---

[81] Adapted from John Pearson's review of *Turning the Flywheel: A Monograph to Accompany Good to Great (Why Some Companies Build Momentum and Others Don't)*, by Jim Collins, *John Pearson's Buckets Blog* (blog), March 19, 2019, https://urgentink.typepad.com/my_weblog/2019/03/turning-the-flywheel.html.

Session 9 ◆ Strategic Planning: Does Your Board Own the Strategy?

BONUS BOOK! Optional Reading!

StrategyMan vs. The Anti-Strategy Squad:
*Using Strategic Thinking
to Defeat Bad Strategy
and Save Your Plan*

by Rich Horwath

True or False?

❑ "A survey of 400 managers found that only 44.3% of organizations have a universal definition of strategy, and less than half (46%) have a common language for strategy."[82]

❑ "A recent study of more than 8,000 new, nationally distributed products found that only 40% were still on the market three years later."[83]

❑ "A survey of nearly 5,000 senior executives showed that more than 50% didn't think they had a winning strategy in place."[84]

---

[82] Rich Horwath, *StrategyMan vs. The Anti-Strategy Squad: Using Strategic Thinking to Defeat Bad Strategy and Save Your Plan* (Austin, TX: Greenleaf Book Group Press, 2018), 21.
[83] Ibid., 72.
[84] Ibid., 117.

SESSION 10

Succession Planning

The Board Should Do What Only the Board Can Do

SESSION 10:
Succession Planning:
The Board Should Do What Only the Board Can Do

> ☑ **HEALTHY GOVERNANCE CHECKLIST**
> CCCA Thriving Boards ◆ Growing Healthy, Effective Boards
>
> **#10. THE BOARD HAS WRITTEN CONTINGENCY PLANS AND SUCCESSION PLANS IN THE EVENT OF A LEADERSHIP TRANSITION (PLANNED OR UNPLANNED).**
> ❏ The full board reviews the written Contingency Plan and written Succession Plan at least annually.
> ❏ The board chair and the CEO regularly affirm that any "elephants in the room" (concerning succession) are appropriately addressed in a timely manner.
> ❏ The full board conducts a CEO performance review at least annually and the CEO recommends a written professional development plan in response to the performance review.
> ❏ The CEO is responsible annually for formally updating the Board on the training, development and leadership potential of all of his/her direct reports, including any high capacity people further down in the organization.

IN THIS SESSION:

❏ 1. A good, simple, communicated <u>Contingency Plan</u> is first.

❏ 2. Develop a written "<u>Draft" Contingency Plan</u>.

❏ 3. A written <u>Succession Plan</u> and the elephant in the room.

Session 10 ◆ Succession Planning

❑ 1. A GOOD, SIMPLE, COMMUNICATED **CONTINGENCY PLAN** IS FIRST.

To get started, answer these questions:

- Who is to take the lead?
  - What are the decision-making parameters?
  - How much money can be spent?

- When and what do we communicate, to whom?
  - Organization
  - Donors
  - Family
  - Insurance – should you have it?
  - Constituents
  - Bank
  - Others?

- What about the organization?
  - Who is in charge?
  - Will we pay them extra?
  - How do we communicate?

- What about the family?
  - Do they know?
  - What can be done to ease the pain?

- Is there an interim leader?

- Do we start a search?

- How is the search to be paid for?

❏ 2. DEVELOP A WRITTEN "DRAFT" CONTINGENCY PLAN.

- Share this Draft Plan with a small group of your most trusted advisors.
- Incorporate their comments into your thinking.
- Work through the plan with your staff, denomination and board.
- Do not try to finish the plan all at once. Think, take your time.
- Make sure it is consistent with your Articles of Incorporation, Bylaws, policies, etc.
- Finalize your "Contingency Plan" and be sure copies are circulated to the people who need to know.
- Think through the benefits or liabilities of sharing your plan within the organization.
- Revisit your Contingency Plan at least annually.

❏ 3. A WRITTEN SUCCESSION PLAN AND THE ELEPHANT IN THE ROOM.

- ❏ **Why so few of us have a good written plan.**
    - Insecurity of the CEO/ED
        - Are they forcing me out?
        - I don't have enough to retire.
        - I am not doing a good job?
        - I haven't had a review in years.

    - Uneasiness from the Board
        - Poor CEO evaluation process, if there is one
        - Marginal performance by the CEO
        - Not wanting to "talk money"
        - Not sure how to create a plan
        - Who should have the conversations?
        - How do we start the conversations without causing concern of the CEO?

- ❏ **Questions to answer:**
    - Do we review the CEO/ED at least annually?
        - Is there a job description in place?
        - Is the succession conversation part of the review?
        - How is a competitive wage established?

    - Is there a process and time table for retirement and/or planned departure?
        - Is there an internal successor(s)?
            - If so, what development needs are there for that person?
            - What training or additional exposure can be offered?
        - If there is not an internal choice, do you have a search firm identified?
            - If not, how do we get started learning about search firms?
        - Who is on the Search Committee?
        - What is our severance policy?
            - ➔ Forced termination?
                - ✓ Performance issues?
                - ✓ For cause?
            - ➔ Unforced termination?
                - ✓ Change in direction for the organization?
                - ✓ Performance not up to expectations?

- ❏ Does the Board have a formal evaluation process in place?
- ❏ Does the Board require SMART Goals be developed and measured annually from the CEO/ED?
- ❏ Is there a Strategic Plan in place?

These questions must be answered by the Board and the CEO/ED. Once answers to these questions are answered, you will have 90% of your Succession Plan complete. Good luck and get started.

RESOURCE: SHORT VIDEO CLIPS AND BLOGS ON SUCCESSION PLANNING

❏ **ECFA Governance Toolbox Series No. 4:**
Succession Planning – 11 Principles for Successful Successions: *"Every CEO is an Interim CEO"*[85]

Each Toolbox includes:
- ❏ Online videos
- ❏ *Board Member Read-and-Engage Viewing Guide*
- ❏ *Facilitator Guide*
- ❏ Access to tools, templates, and resources on hidden webpage

www.ecfa.org/toolbox
Contact CCCA Thriving Boards for promo code

BLOG POSTS ON TOOLBOX NO. 4: John Pearson wrote a series of 11 blog posts for ECFA on each of the 11 principles in Toolbox No. 4. Visit ECFA's "Governance of Christ-Centered Organizations" blog at:
http://ecfagovernance.blogspot.com/2018/06/succession-planning-11-principles-index.html

❏ **Principle No. 1:** Avoid Buses and Boredom! - "My Heart Had Left the Building"

❏ **Principle No. 2:** Discern Your Board's Succession Values and Beliefs - "Appointment Without Anointment Always Led to Disaster"

❏ **Principle No. 3:** Inspire Your CEO to Thrive With a God-Honoring Lifestyle – "Is Your CEO Thriving or Just Surviving?"

❏ **Principle No. 4:** Model Successful Succession in the Boardroom First - "'One Size Fits All' Is Bad Counsel"

❏ **Principle No. 5:** Delegate Succession Planning to the Appropriate Committee – "The Ongoing Continuous Process"

❏ **Principle No. 6:** Invest in Growing Your Leaders (Every Leader Needs a Coach) – "Does Your CEO Need a Coach?"

❏ **Principle No. 7:** Trust God and Discern Direction! Wisdom on Ending Well - "Wise People Know When to Quit"

❏ **Principle No. 8** - Plan for Plan A: Your CEO Retires - "Do I Still Have Fire in My Belly?"

❏ **Principle No. 9** - Plan for Plan B: Your CEO Resigns – "The Five Stages of CEO Abandonment"

❏ **Principle No. 10** - Plan for Plan C: Your CEO Is Terminated – "Hire Slower and Fire Faster"

❏ **Principle No. 11** – Discern If a Search Firm Would Be Helpful – "Differences Between Search Firms"[86]

---

[85] *ECFA Governance Toolbox Series No. 4: Succession Planning – 11 Principles for Successful Successions:* "Every CEO is an Interim CEO" *(Winchester, VA: ECFAPress, 2017) – www.ECFA.org/toolbox*

[86] *John Pearson,* "Succession Planning: 11 Principles (Index to 11 Blogs)," *Governance of Christ-Centered Organizations (blog), June 11, 2018,* http://ecfagovernance.blogspot.com/2018/06/succession-planning-11-principles-index.html.

SESSION 11

Strategic Next Steps and My One Big Take-Away

SESSION 11:
Strategic Next Steps and My One Big Take-Away (following the Fall Session)

IN THIS SESSION:

❑ 1. <u>Personal</u>: My One Big Take-Away

❑ 2. <u>With Your Coach</u>: Coaching Process Options

❑ 3. <u>Memo to Executive Director</u>: "Our Top-5 Strategic Next Steps"

HENRY BLACKABY
"God reveals His will and invites you to join Him where He is already at work."[87]

WINSTON CHURCHILL
"There is in the act of preparing, the moment you start caring."

GARY KELLER
"What's the ONE Thing you can do this week such that by doing it everything else would be easier or unnecessary?"[88]

---

[87] Henry T. Blackaby and Claude V. King, *Experiencing God: Knowing and Doing the Will of God* (Nashville: LifeWay Press, 1990), 8.

[88] Gary Keller with Jay Papasan, *The ONE Thing: The Surprisingly Simple Truth Behind Extraordinary Results* (Austin, TX: Bard, 2012), 114. (Note: the authors suggest you ask this question of seven areas of your life: …for my spiritual life, …for my business, …for my job, etc.)

Session 11 ◆ Strategic Next Steps and My One Big Take-Away

❑ 1. PERSONAL: MY ONE BIG TAKE-AWAY

My Name: _____
➔ Share Your One Big Take-Away (at your table):

1	

Session 11 ◆ Strategic Next Steps and My One Big Take-Away

❏ 2. WITH YOUR COACH: COACHING PROCESS OPTIONS
(more details will be presented in this session)

Our Coach is: _____

Two Days of Coaching Provided by CCCA With Flexible Options!
  ❏ One day on-site: _____, 20_____
  ❏ One day for projects, phone coaching, etc.
   (or a second day on-site, later in the year, with travel covered by our camp)

  ❏ Two days on-site: _____, 20_____

Review the following pages to discern where your coach may be of help to you:

SECTION A: BOARD ENRICHMENT/TRAINING

✓	COACH THE BOARD AND/OR CEO, OR COMMITTEE, ON YOUR MOST STRATEGIC NEXT STEPS:

Place an * by the three most strategic next steps.

Session 11 ◆ Strategic Next Steps and My One Big Take-Away

SECTION B: DOCUMENTS/COACHING

PRIORITY: A B C	TOOLS and TEMPLATES ☑ = Top-5 Tools to begin using this month	TARGET DATE	POINT PERSON
	❏ Tool #1: The Pathway to the Board		
	❏ Tool #2: Board Nominee Suggestion Form		
	❏ Tool #3: Board Nominee Orientation: Table of Contents		
	❏ Tool #4: Five-Finger Feedback		
	❏ Tool #5: Board's Annual Self-Assessment Survey		
	❏ Tool #6: The Board's Annual Financial Management Audit		
	❏ Tool #7: The Board's Annual Legal Audit		
	❏ Tool #8: The Board's Annual Fundraising Audit		
	❏ Tool #9: The Board's Annual Evaluation of the Top Leader		
	❏ Tool #10: The 5/15 Monthly Report to the Board		
	❏ Tool #11: Monthly Dashboard Report		
	❏ Tool #12: Quarterly Board Meeting Agenda & Recommendations		
	❏ Tool #13: Board Retreat Read-and-Reflect Worksheets		
	❏ Tool #14: The Rolling 3-Year Strategic Plan Placemat		
	❏ Tool #15: Board Retreat Trend-Spotting Exercise		
	❏ Tool #16: Prime Responsibility Chart		
	❏ Tool #17: Board Policies Manual (BPM)		
	❏ Tool #18: Job Descriptions for the Top Leader and Board Chair		
	❏ Tool #19: Ten Minutes for Governance		
	❏ Tool #20: Tent Cards and Tools for Leveraging Board Strengths		
	❏ Tool #21: Board Member Annual Affirmation Statement		
	❏ Tool #22: Straw Vote Cards		

➔**Reminder!** If you, or your organization, purchased this book (or received it as part of a board training/enrichment experience), you are authorized to download the templates. (See the templates webpage and password on the title page of the book.)

---

[89] Busby and Pearson, *ECFA Tools and Templates for Effective Board Governance*

Session 11 ♦ Strategic Next Steps and My One Big Take-Away

SECTION C: "DAVE COLEMAN'S "BOARD ESSENTIALS LIST"

☑	FROM: BOARD ESSENTIALS 12 BEST PRACTICES OF NONPROFIT BOARDS

Dave Coleman's
"POTENTIAL ACTION STRATEGIES FOR BOARD ENGAGEMENT COACHING" [90]

MEMBERSHIP

#1 Boards are passionately mission focused
- ___ Organization Vision, Mission, and Value Statements
- ___ Standardized Elevator Speech
- ___ Plan to Better Connect Board Members to the Mission and Programs

#2 Boards are right-sized with quality members and relationships
- ___ Updated By-Laws
- ___ Committee Development
- ___ Place Board Members and their terms (# term, year elected) in writing
- ___ Written Process and Strategy for Board Recruitment and Selection
- ___ Board Membership Strengths Assessment and Follow-up Discussion
- ___ Written Board Membership Criteria
- ___ "Farm System" for Cultivating Potential Board Members
- ___ Development of a Board Orientation and Engagement Strategy

#3 Boards understand and are effective at governance
- ___ Review and Discuss the Legal Duties of a Board
- ___ Board Member Conflict of Interest Policy and Statement (to be signed)

#4 Boards and their members are clear about their roles and responsibilities
- ___ Written Board Roles
- ___ Written Board Member Responsibilities and Expectations
- ___ Customized Annual Board Member Job Descriptions
- ___ Board Member Annual Affirmation

---

[90] David L. Coleman, *Board Essentials: 12 Best Practices of Nonprofit Boards* (Tacoma, WA: Andrew/Wallace Books, 2014), 9-12.

LEADERSHIP

#5 Boards supervise only the CEO
- ___ CEO/ Executive Director Job Description
- ___ Clarity in the Board-CEO Relationship
- ___ CEO/ Executive Director Annual Goals and Work Plan
- ___ CEO/Executive Director Annual Performance Review Plan
- ___ Succession Discussion and Planning ("In the event of...")

#6 Boards have an effective CEO-Board Chair partnership
- ___ CEO-Board Information Management System
- ___ Board Chair Job Description
- ___ CEO – Board Chair Partnership Plan

DECISIONS

#7 Boards focus on policy, and thereby speak with one voice
- ___ Assessment of Board Interaction
- ___ Identify All Board Approved Policies

#8 Boards function with clear processes for meetings
- ___ Coaching for Better Board Meetings
- ___ Upgraded Board Meeting Agenda
- ___ Development of a Consent Agenda
- ___ Board Meeting Protocols (Rules of the Road)
- ___ Board Meeting Follow-up Strategy
- ___ Develop Relationship Building Strategies for Board Members
- ___ Conflict Resolution
- ___ Implement an Annual Board Retreat

#9 Boards give attention to the future, end results, and big issues
- ___ Clarity and Focus Workshop (1 page summer; based on Patrick Lencioni's *The Advantage*)
- ___ Board Discussion – From Micro to Macro as a Board Role
- ___ Development of a Strategic Plan
- ___ Development of Board Approved Annual Goals for the Organization
- ___ Strategy for Utilizing the Strategic Plan and Goals
- ___ Board Education related to the Organization's Sector and Environment
- ___ Generative Discussion Related to the Organization and the Future
- ___ Identification of "Game Changers" Internally and Externally

#10 Boards exercise fiduciary responsibility
- ___ Risk Management Audit
- ___ Creation of Risk Management Policies
- ___ Crisis Management and Public Interaction Plan
- ___ Creation of a Finance Committee
- ___ Creation of an Audit Committee (separate from Finance Committee)
- ___ Adoption of a set of Financial Policies
- ___ Unrestricted Cash Requirements and Policies
- ___ Internal audit of Financial Practices and Follow-up Action Steps

____ Upgrade of Budget Practices
____ Upgrade of Financial Reporting
____ Education of the Board on Understanding Financial Statements
____ Annual CPA Compilation, Review, or Audit: Decision on What is Best for Us
____ Creation of a Financial Dashboard
____ Creation of a Fundraising Dashboard
____ Strategy for Board Engagement in Fundraising

#11 Boards govern with a fluid and concise "Board Policy Manual"
____ Creation of a Board Policy Notebook
____ Development of a Board Policy Manual (BPM)
____ Creation of a BPM Implementation Plan
____ Creation of a Board Compliance Strategy

#12 Boards have an active year round board development committee
____ Upgrade Current Governance Committee
____ Identification of a Board Member with a Special Interest in Board Health
____ Creation of a Board Development Committee
____ Inclusion of a Board Line Item in the Budget

NOTES:

❏ 3. Memo to Executive Director: "Our Top-5 Strategic Next Steps"

"OUR TOP-5 STRATEGIC NEXT STEPS"

MEMO

TO:	**Executive Directors of Participating Camps** **CCCA THRIVING BOARDS**
FROM:	Ed McDowell *Project Coordinator*
RE:	Thriving Boards Program: Strategic Next Steps

Attached is a document, **"Our Top-5 Strategic Next Steps."** Based on the work you accomplished during the Fall Session, please complete the worksheet and HAND DELIVER IT. We will arrange to make a copy for both you and your coach.

Your list does not need to be perfect or absolutely your final/final "Top-5." But, hopefully, it will reflect the good work, discussion, interaction and discernment you engaged in together.

Please submit this during Session 11:

	3 OPTIONS	See flipchart in meeting room:
Option 1:	Hand Deliver	To:
Option 2:	Email the digital Word document	Email:
Option 3:	Email a photo of your list	Mobile:

Session 11 ◆ Strategic Next Steps and My One Big Take-Away

"OUR TOP-5 STRATEGIC NEXT STEPS"

3 OPTIONS→ Hand Deliver, Email the Digital Document, or Email Photo of Document

Camp/Conference Center	
Executive Director	
Name of person who completed this form:	
Today's date:	

As a result of our participation in the Fall Session of the CCCA THRIVING BOARDS program, here are our "Top-5 Strategic Next Steps" related to board leadership and development.

Top-5 Strategic Next Steps – Board Leadership and Development

POINT PERSON	STRATEGIC NEXT STEPS	NEED COACH'S HELP?	DEADLINE	DONE DATE
	1)	❑ Yes ❑ No		
	2)	❑ Yes ❑ No		
	3)	❑ Yes ❑ No		
	4)	❑ Yes ❑ No		
	5)	❑ Yes ❑ No		

SESSION 12

Reporting In: Organizational Progress Reports

SPRING SESSION WELCOME BACK!

SESSION 12:
Reporting In: Organizational Progress Reports

IN THIS SESSION:

❑ 1. <u>Welcome Back</u>! Introduction of New Participants and Guests

❑ 2. <u>Spring Session</u>! Brief Overview and Prayer

❑ 3. <u>Breakouts</u>! With Your Coach – Update on Your "Top-5 Strategic Next Steps"

"EVERYTHING IS FINE!"

Excerpt from a review of *Scaling Up*:

As an example of the helpful detail on meetings, Harnish drops in frequent warning icons. "What's the rock in your shoe?" is a high priority meeting agenda question for the daily huddle.
- ☑ Where are you stuck?
- ☑ What constraints are you facing in the next 24 hours?
- ☑ And this wisdom/warning:

"**WARNING:** Anytime somebody goes two days without reporting a constraint, you can bet there's a problem lurking. Busy, productive people who are doing anything of consequence get stuck pretty regularly. **The only people who don't get stuck are those who aren't doing anything or are so stuck that they don't know it!!** So, challenge the team member who reports, 'Everything is fine!'" (See page 183.)[91]

---

[91] *John Pearson,* "Sloppy Execution and Lack of Discipline: *Scaling Up* [review], *John Pearson's Buckets Blog*, Dec. 14, 2018, https://urgentink.typepad.com/my_weblog/2018/12/scaling-up-rockefeller-habits-20.html.

❏ 3. BREAKOUTS! WITH YOUR COACH

Update: "Top-5 Strategic Next Steps"

TOP-5 STRATEGIC NEXT STEPS

POINT PERSON	STRATEGIC NEXT STEPS	NEED COACH'S HELP?	DEADLINE	DONE DATE
	1)	❏ Yes ❏ No		
	2)	❏ Yes ❏ No		
	3)	❏ Yes ❏ No		
	4)	❏ Yes ❏ No		
	5)	❏ Yes ❏ No		

SESSION 13

The Board's Financial/Fiduciary Roles

The BPM Practicum

SESSION 13:
The Board's Financial/Fiduciary Roles: The BPM Practicum

☑ HEALTHY GOVERNANCE CHECKLIST
CCCA Thriving Boards ◆ Growing Healthy, Effective Boards

#13. BOARD MEMBERS ARE DILIGENT IN THEIR FIDUCIARY GOVERNANCE ROLES.
- ❏ The board's governance documents clearly articulate the financial, legal, and fiduciary roles of board members.
- ❏ Board members trust God as they steward their fiduciary governance roles and responsibilities, especially related to the bylaws; local, state, and federal laws and regulations; financial audits and program audits; financial controls and cash reserves; CEO compensation-setting policies; accreditation; and other written responsibilities.
- ❏ The board regularly updates the *Board Policies Manual (BPM)* or a similar policy document.
- ❏ The board ensures that the CEO and financial team are focused on "The 7 Key Financial Levers."[92]

IN THIS SESSION:

❏ 1. <u>Overview</u>: Three Aspects of Governance: Fiduciary, Strategic, Generative

❏ 2. <u>Exercise</u>: The Board Policies Manual (BPM) Practicum – Executive Parameters

❏ 3. <u>Presentation</u>: *Scaling Up* (15 Minutes Including Q & A)

"We need to do everything God wants us to do."

Check out the 100 quotations on trust, compiled by Dan Busby:[93]

- ❏ "Our problem as leaders is we do everything we know to do. That's not enough. We need to do everything God wants us to do." (Richard Blackaby)
- ❏ "A Christ-centered ministry that lacks trust is like a teenager running through a fireworks factory with a lit blowtorch. It isn't whether something is going to blow up—it's just a matter of when." (Busby)
- ❏ "Leadership is an achievement of trust." (Peter F. Drucker)
- ❏ "Trust is the starting point for all healthy relationships, the fuel for team ministry, and the cornerstone of group effectiveness." (Stephen Macchia)
- ❏ "Trust is the emotional glue that binds followers and leaders together." (Warren G. Bennis)
- ❏ "The perception of a conflict of interest can be just as damaging to a ministry's reputation as an actual conflict." (Busby)

http://www.ecfa.org/Trust/QuotableQuotes.aspx

---

[92] See page 231 in *Scaling Up*, by Verne Harnish, and read "The Power of One and the 7 Levers" which include: 1) Price, 2) Volume, 3) Costs of goods sold/direct costs, 4) Operating expenses, 5) Accounts receivable, 6) Inventory/work in progress, and 7) Accounts payable.

[93] Dan Busby, *Trust: The Firm Foundation for Kingdom Fruitfulness* (Winchester, VA: ECFAPress, 2015).

Session 13 ◆ The Board's Financial/Fiduciary Role: The BPM Practicum

❑ 1. OVERVIEW: THREE ASPECTS OF GOVERNANCE: FIDUCIARY, STRATEGIC, GENERATIVE

Prudent Person Rule

"In general, board members are legally held accountable to the principle of the 'Prudent Person Rule.' This essentially means they are expected to perform within the bounds of what any reasonably intelligent and prudent person would be expected to do (or not to do) in managing or investing his or her own funds in similar circumstances.

"This is not an unreasonable expectation **and should not cause us to lose sleep at night.** But it does require reasonable due diligence on our part as board members by asking the right questions at the right time."[94]

TEN BASIC RESPONSIBILITIES OF NONPROFIT BOARDS[95]
1. Determine mission and purpose, and advocate for them
2. Select the chief executive
3. Support and evaluate the chief executive
4. Ensure effective planning
5. Monitor and strengthen programs and services
☑ 6. Ensure adequate financial resources
☑ 7. Protect assets and provide financial oversight
8. Build a competent board
☑ 9. Ensure legal and ethical integrity
10. Enhance the organization's public standing

QUICK QUIZ: THREE ASPECTS OF GOVERNANCE. How strongly do you agree with the following questions about your board's effectiveness in these three aspects of governance? (See next pages for definitions.)

☑ THREE ASPECTS OF GOVERNANCE	5 Strongly Agree	4 Agree	3 Undecided	2 Disagree	1 Strongly Disagree	Weighted Average
Our board is very effective in **FIDUCIARY** governance.						
Our board is very effective in **STRATEGIC** governance.						
Our board is very effective in **GENERATIVE** governance.						

---

[94] Richard T. Ingram, *Ten Basic Responsibilities of Nonprofit Boards, Third Edition*, (Washington, DC: BoardSource, 2015), 62.
[95] Ibid., v-vi.

ECFA GOVERNANCE SURVEY: HIGHLIGHT #4. In rating effectiveness relative to the three essential aspects of governance, fiduciary governance rated highest, but generative governance rated the lowest.

Board members agree that they are very effective in their "Fiduciary Governance" roles, but much less effective in their "Generative Governance" roles—the re-imagining of the organization, in light of trends and opportunities.

THE THREE ASPECTS OF GOVERNANCE

The percentage of board members who AGREE or STRONGLY AGREE that "our board is very effective" in these three aspects of governance:

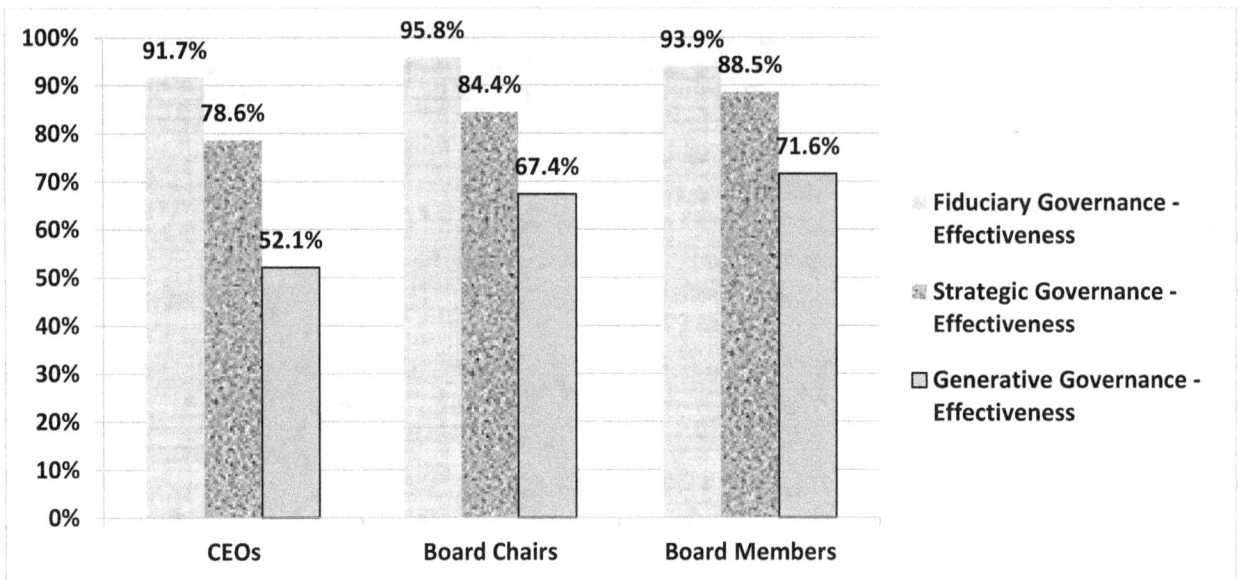

INSIGHT: Board chairs and board members rate their effectiveness in these three aspects of governance higher than do CEOs. While all three groups rated "Fiduciary Governance" high (from 92% to 96%), the ratings for "Generative Governance" were much lower and with a wider range (from 52% to 72%).

Governance as Leadership: Reframing the Work of Nonprofit Boards, identifies three aspects of governance:[96]

✓ **FIDUCIARY GOVERNANCE:** due diligence, audits, CEO compensation, bylaws, financial controls, etc.

✓ **STRATEGIC GOVERNANCE:** ensuring that programs are in alignment with the mission, vision, and core values; and that there is a strategic planning process in place.

✓ **GENERATIVE GOVERNANCE:** often overlooked, broader re-imagining of the organization's nature and role in light of emerging trends; here board members also explore "opportunities to be a source of leadership as well as a source of advice, expertise, and fundraising."

---

[96] Richard P. Chait, William P. Ryan, and Barbara E. Taylor, *Governance as Leadership*, 6-7.

Session 13 ◆ The Board's Financial/Fiduciary Role: The BPM Practicum

☐ 2. **EXERCISE:**
THE BOARD POLICIES MANUAL (BPM) PRACTICUM - EXECUTIVE PARAMETERS

Board Policies Manual:
A 10- to 15-page Template to Customize Based on Your Unique Needs

Good Governance for Nonprofits: Developing Principles and Policies for an Effective Board[97]
by Fredric L. Laughlin and Robert C. Andringa

- ❑ Focuses on a 10- to 15-page document with all board policies
- ❑ Color commentary on each policy
- ❑ Designed to be updated frequently, based on organizational needs and changing internal and external realities
- ❑ Simpler and more time-saving alternative to other policy approaches
- ❑ Although this is not designed as a "faith-based" BPM, the context is built in so you can add the Christ-centered distinctives of your ministry.

☑	**TEMPLATE DOWNLOAD OPTIONS:**
	#1. Access the password in your organization's copy of: ***ECFA Tools and Templates for Effective Board Governance: Time-Saving Solutions for Your Board*** ☑ Tool: Board Policies Manual (BPM)
	#2. Visit Bob Andringa's website for the latest template: https://theandringagroup.com/resources/
	#3. Contact CCCA Thriving Boards → Note: Previous versions of this workbook have listed the AMACOM website, but books by AMA are now being distributed by HarperCollins Leadership. As of press time, their website does not offer downloads of the template.

---

[97] Fredric L. Laughlin and Robert C. Andringa, *Good Governance for Nonprofits*

Session 13 ◆ The Board's Financial/Fiduciary Role: The BPM Practicum

WORKSHEET/EXERCISE:

Assignment: Begin Work on Section 5 of the Board Policies Manual (BPM)
➔ Note: The full BPM can be downloaded from your organization's copy of the book, *ECFA Tools and Templates for Effective Board Governance.*

For a color commentary on "Part 5: Executive Parameters," (and commentaries on each section) consult the book,
Good Governance for Nonprofits

Use by permission of Bob Andringa and Fred Laughlin, co-authors.
https://theandringagroup.com/resources/

PART 5: EXECUTIVE PARAMETERS

5.1 General Guidance. The purpose of the remainder of the BPM is to detail those executive parameters that will guide the CEO and the staff as they accomplish the mission. These parameters are intended to free the CEO and the staff to make timely decisions without undue board directives. The board expects that the CEO will do nothing that is illegal, unethical, or imprudent. Beyond these general parameters, the board details its executive parameters in the major sections that follow in Part 5.

5.2 Finance Parameters. The CEO must ensure that the financial integrity of the organization is maintained at all times; that proper care is exercised in the receiving, processing, and disbursing of funds; and that financial and nonfinancial assets are appropriately protected.

5.2.1 Budgeting. The budget during any fiscal period shall not (a) deviate materially from the board's goals and priorities listed in Part 2, (b) risk fiscal jeopardy, or (c) fail to show a generally acceptable level of foresight. Accordingly, the CEO may not cause or allow budgeting that:

5.2.1.1 Contains too little detail to (a) enable accurate projection of revenues and expenses, (b) separate capital items from operational items, (c) monitor cash flow and subsequent audit trails, and (d) disclose planning assumptions.

5.2.1.2 Anticipates the expenditure in any fiscal year of more funds than are conservatively projected to be received in that period.

5.2.1.3 Reduces the current assets at any time to less than twice current liabilities or allows cash to drop below a safety reserve of $_____ at any time.

5.2.1.4 Provides less than $_____ for board prerogatives during the year, such as costs of the annual audit and board development.

5.2.1.5 Is not derived from the strategic plan.

5.2.2 Financial Controls. The CEO must exercise care in accounting for and protecting the financial assets of the organization. To this end, the CEO is expected to incorporate generally accepted accounting principles and internal controls in the financial systems that are employed in the organization. In addition, the CEO may not:

5.2.2.1 Receive, process, or disburse funds under controls insufficient to meet the board-appointed auditor's standards.

5.2.2.2 Approve an unbudgeted expenditure or commitment of greater than $_____ without the approval of the full board.

5.2.2.3 Approve an unbudgeted expenditure or commitment of greater than $_____ without the approval of the Finance Committee.

5.2.3 Asset Protection. The CEO may not allow assets to be unprotected, inadequately maintained, or unnecessarily risked. Accordingly, the CEO may not:

5.2.3.1 Fail to insure against theft and casualty losses to at least 80 percent of replacement cost and against liability losses to board members, staff, or the organization itself beyond the minimally acceptable prudent level.

5.2.3.2 Allow non-bonded personnel access to material amounts of funds.

5.2.3.3 Subject office equipment to improper wear and tear or insufficient maintenance.

5.2.3.4 Unnecessarily expose the organization, its board, or its staff to claims of liability.

5.2.3.5 Make any major purchase of over $_____ without sealed bids or some other demonstrably prudent method of acquisition of quality goods, or any purchase of over $_____ without a written record of competitive prices, or any purchase wherein normally prudent protection against conflict of interest has not been provided.

5.2.3.6 Acquire, encumber, or dispose of real property without board approval.

5.2.4 Investment Principles. The CEO may not invest or hold operating capital in insecure instruments, including uninsured checking accounts and bonds of less than AA rating, or in non-interest-bearing accounts, except where necessary to facilitate operational transactions.

5.3 Program Parameters. In general, the CEO is expected to establish, maintain, and eliminate programs and services to achieve the organization's mission and goals in the most effective and efficient manner.

5.3.1 New programs should be projected to serve at least _____ people.

5.3.2 New programs with an expected budget exceeding $_____ must be approved by the board. Those programs now approved include:

5.3.3 Programs with costs of more than $____ shall be assessed for effectiveness by an outside evaluator at least every three years, with a written report being made available to the board.

5.3.4   Any program executed in partnership with another organization shall _____.

5.4   Advancement Parameters. The various efforts to represent the organization to the public (media, public relations, fund-raising, new member recruitment, etc.) shall be integrated sufficiently that the organization's brand/positioning in the external world is positive and effective.

5.4.1   **Fund-Raising Strategy.** The CEO shall develop and maintain a fund-raising plan that, at a minimum, includes direct mail, major donor initiatives, planned giving, and web-based giving. Such plan shall be provided to board members for review each March, along with results for each initiative. Total direct and indirect expenses for fund-raising shall not exceed 22 percent of the total budget.

5.4.1.1 **Donor Bill of Rights.** The CEO shall develop a Donor Bill of Rights and provide the latest version to the board; this shall include, *inter alia*, the following restrictions: the CEO may not allow the names of donors to be revealed outside the organization, represent to a donor that an action will be taken that violates board policies, fail to honor a request from a donor as to how her/his contribution is to be allocated, fail to confirm receipt of a donor's contribution, or fail to send a donor an annual summary of donations.

5.4.1.2 **Training.** The CEO shall ensure that appropriate members of the board and staff receive annual training in new fund-raising techniques and shall budget for such expenses.

5.4.2   **Public Affairs.** The CEO shall exercise care in representing that we are a charitable, mission-centered, listening organization and shall develop policies and procedures for communicating with primary stakeholders and the public at large in a way that reinforces that image.

5.4.2.1 **Communications Plan.** The CEO shall develop and maintain a communications plan, shared with the board as appropriate, that describes how the organization will communicate with its various stakeholders. The plan shall identify the stakeholder segments, how the organization will both speak and listen to each segment, and who is allowed to speak for the organization. The plan shall also include the role of board members both as "listeners" and as "speakers" for the organization.

5.4.2.2 **Communications Restrictions.** To preserve our image in the community, the CEO and any designee are the only spokespersons authorized to speak for the organization, and the chair is the only spokesperson for the board. None of the spokespersons may represent the organization in any way that is inconsistent with the policies in Part 2 of this BPM; make statements that may be perceived as supporting a political party or platform; be the author of an article, book, or publication that includes classified or sensitive information about the organization; or engage in lobbying activities at any governmental level without prior permission from the board.

5.5   Audit and Compliance Parameters. The CEO shall take the necessary steps to ensure the integrity of our systems and procedures; to see that they comply with all pertinent legal, regulatory, and professional requirements; and to report to the board any material variations or violations.

5.5.1 **Annual External Audit.** An independent auditor will be hired and supervised by the Audit and Compliance Committee, after a careful selection and annual evaluation. The CEO shall work with the auditor to gain a clean opinion on the annual financial statements and respond in detail to items in the auditor's management letter concerning opportunities to improve systems and procedures related to financial controls.

5.5.2 **Internal Compliance.** The CEO shall meet all requirements for complying with federal, state, or local laws and regulations. The CEO shall maintain a list of compliance actions and reports that are required of a nonprofit organization and periodically submit the list for inspection by the Audit and Compliance Committee. On a biennial basis, starting in _____, the CEO shall contract for a legal review of the organization's compliance with the pertinent laws and regulations and make the results of the review available to the Audit and Compliance Committee, which, in turn, will report to the board on the overall status of the organization with respect to compliance matters, including any current problems or anticipated problems with regulatory authorities.

5.6   **Miscellaneous.** [Include other policies that don't naturally fit into one of the other major sections.]

Session 13 ◆ The Board's Financial/Fiduciary Role: The BPM Practicum

❑ 3. PRESENTATION: *SCALING UP* (15 MINUTES INCLUDING Q & A)

Presenter	
Scaling Up Chapter	14. THE POWER OF ONE: 7 Key Financial Levers
#1. The big idea for our staff is:	
#2. The big idea for our board is:	
#3. I'm guessing that your biggest question about this chapter is:	

SCALING UP:
How a Few Companies
Make It...and
Why the Rest Don't
Mastering the Rockefeller Habits 2.0
by Verne Harnish

SCALING UP: THE POWER OF ONE AND THE 7 FINANCIAL LEVERS (p. 231) [98]

NO.	THE 7 FINANCIAL LEVERS	NOTES
1	Price	
2	Volume	
3	Cost of goods sold (COGS)/direct costs	
4	Operating expenses	
5	Accounts receivable	
6	Inventory/work in progress	
7	Accounts payable	

---

[98] Verne Harnish, *Scaling Up*, 231.

SESSION 14

The Board's Financial/Fiduciary Role:

Long-term Sustainability

a.k.a.
Would a foundation view your organization as floundering or flourishing?

SESSION 14:
The Board's Financial/Fiduciary Role: Long-term Sustainability

> **☑ HEALTHY GOVERNANCE CHECKLIST**
> CCCA Thriving Boards ◆ Growing Healthy, Effective Boards
>
> **#14. THE BOARD MONITORS BOTH FINANCIAL AND PROGRAMMATIC HEALTH.**
> ❑ The board regularly reviews key indicators of financial health—and the importance and status of cash.
> ❑ The board regularly reviews key indicators that measure the health of the organization's programs, products, and services.
> ❑ The board affirms the organization's Business Model Statement.
> ❑ The board appropriately balances mission impact and sustainability—and discerns the organization's budget, and program priorities in light of Kingdom impact.

➔KEY OUTCOMES FOR THIS SESSION:
What are the appropriate questions for the board to be asking regarding sustainability?

IN THIS SESSION:

❑ 1. Discuss: The concept of sustainability as it relates to the life of your organization.

❑ 2. Exercise: Brainstorm a list of areas that camps may need to address regarding sustainability. Identify which of these areas your board needs to address in the next 3-5 years to ensure your organization's sustainability.

❑ 3. Discuss: Learn why "sustainability" is so important for your board and staff, for foundations, and most importantly for the Kingdom! (Luke 14:28-30)

❑ 4. Inside the Mind of a Foundation: Insights into indicators of financial and programmatic health

❑ 5. Exercise: Consider your board's role in ensuring the sustainability of your organization.

❑ 6. Tools: Look at sustainability through the filter of two helpful resources: *Scaling Up* and *The Nonprofit Strategy Revolution*.

❑ 7. Homework Exercise from Session 9: Note! This was your "homework exercise" from Session 9. **Purpose:** Learn how to create a matrix map for your organization. Once completed, this will provide insights for making strategic decisions for financial viability. (Worksheets #4 to 9)

❑ 8. Presentation: *Scaling Up* (15 Minutes Including Q & A) – "The 7 Strata of Strategy"

Session 14 ◆ The Board's Financial/Fiduciary Role: Long-Term Sustainability

❑ 1. DISCUSS: THE CONCEPT OF SUSTAINABILITY AS IT RELATES TO THE LIFE OF YOUR ORGANIZATION

QUESTION: What does sustainability mean to our organization?	ANSWER:

Defining Two Areas of Sustainability:

- Financial Sustainability: the ability to generate resources to meet the needs of the present without compromising the future
- Programmatic Sustainability: the ability to develop, mature, and cycle out programs to be responsive to constituencies over time

❑ 2. EXERCISE: BRAINSTORM A LIST OF AREAS THAT CAMPS MAY NEED TO ADDRESS REGARDING SUSTAINABILITY. Identify which of these areas your board needs to address in the next 3-5 years to ensure your organization's sustainability.

WORKSHEET #1:

#1. In the table below, list potential areas that camps may need to address regarding sustainability.
#2. Then identify and prioritize the top-5 areas of greatest need for your board to address in the next 3-5 years.

SUSTAINABILITY AREAS	PRIORITY

Session 14 ◆ The Board's Financial/Fiduciary Role: Long-Term Sustainability

❑ **3. DISCUSS:** LEARN WHY "SUSTAINABILITY" IS SO IMPORTANT FOR YOUR BOARD AND STAFF, FOR FOUNDATIONS, AND MOST IMPORTANTLY FOR THE KINGDOM! (LUKE 14:28-30)

WHY IS SUSTAINABILITY SO IMPORTANT?

For your board and staff?

For foundations and donors?

For constituents?

For the Kingdom? (Luke 14:28-30)

"Is there anyone here who, planning to build a new house, doesn't first sit down and figure the cost so you'll know if you can complete it? If you only get the foundation laid and then run out of money, you're going to look pretty foolish. Everyone passing by will poke fun at you: 'He started something he couldn't finish.'"

Luke 14:28-30 (*The Message*)

❑ 4. INSIDE THE MIND OF A FOUNDATION:
INSIGHTS INTO INDICATORS OF FINANCIAL AND PROGRAMMATIC HEALTH

a.k.a.
➔ **Would a foundation view your organization as floundering or flourishing?**

Foundations (and major donors) considering a funding request from your organization will likely examine the overall health and potential sustainability of your organization as part of their due diligence prior to providing any support. These funders want to know that they are investing in a going concern and that the project they are helping is also sustainable. There are a variety of areas related to sustainability which camps face that funders will inquire about—including the following two areas of board responsibility that will always be examined:
- sustaining financial health
- and sustaining mission impact over time.

➔ **Would a foundation evaluate your financial picture as healthy?**

WORKSHEET #2: INDICATORS OF A HEALTHY FINANCIAL PICTURE:

#1. List potential indicators of a healthy financial picture.
#2. Identify related Red Flags for each indicator.
#3. Rate your organization for each indicator on the following scale:

1 = Emerging..5 = Mature/Solid

INDICATORS	RED FLAGS	RATING 1 - 5

Zone of Insolvency: How Nonprofits Avoid Hidden Liabilities and Build Financial Strength, by Ron Mattocks

• "The Zone of Insolvency is a period of corporate financial distress, sandwiched between solvency and total insolvency."[99]
• "If we decided today to close this organization, would we complete the close-down with net assets remaining, or net liability?"[100]

---

[99] Ron Mattocks, *Zone of Insolvency: How Nonprofits Avoid Hidden Liabilities and Build Financial Strength* (Hoboken, NJ: John Wiley and Sons, Inc., 2008), xxi.
[100] Ibid., 135.

WORKSHEET #3:

INDICATORS OF A HEALTHY PROGRAMMATIC PICTURE:

#1. List indicators of healthy programs for a camp or conference center.
#2. Rate your organization for each indicator on the following scale:

1 = Emerging……………………………………………………………..…………**5 = Mature/Solid**

INDICATORS	RATING 1 - 5

Session 14 ◆ The Board's Financial/Fiduciary Role: Long-Term Sustainability

❑ 5. EXERCISE: CONSIDER YOUR BOARD'S ROLE IN ENSURING SUSTAINABILITY OF YOUR ORGANIZATION.

☑ CHECKLIST: The Board's Role in Ensuring Sustainability	True/False	How does the board know?
The board receives the necessary data in a timely manner to provide board level policy decisions regarding financial matters.		
The board's financial oversight supports our sustainability.		
The board receives the necessary information to steward the spiritual side of the ministry.		
The board receives the necessary data to determine the degree of mission impact of our programs and activities.		
Other:		
Other:		
Other:		

☑ TRUE
☐ FALSE

MORE CHECKLISTS:
See additional True/False checklists in *ECFA Tools and Templates for Effective Board Governance.*

Session 14 ◆ The Board's Financial/Fiduciary Role: Long-Term Sustainability

❏ **6. TOOLS: LOOK AT SUSTAINABILITY THROUGH THE FILTER OF TWO HELPFUL RESOURCES:** *SCALING UP* **AND** *THE NONPROFIT STRATEGY REVOLUTION.* Consider additional perspectives/strategies for your boards to consider as you examine your role in shepherding/ensuring the sustainability of the organization.

SCALING UP KEY QUESTION:
"Do you have consistent sources of cash, ideally generated internally, to fuel the growth of your business?"

"You can get by with decent People, Strategy, and Execution, but not a day without Cash."[101]

The Nonprofit Strategy Revolution: Real-Time Strategic Planning in a Rapid-Response World, by David La Piana

Winston Churchill: "However beautiful the strategy, you should occasionally look at the results."[102]

➜ This book includes access to 27 tools for forming strategy, including "Tool 1: Current Business Model."

PLUS! THIS BONUS BOOK:

Nonprofit Sustainability:
Making Strategic Decisions for Financial Viability
by Jeanne Bell, Jan Masaoka and Steve Zimmerman

"Locating activities in these quadrants—what we call creating a Matrix Map—will suggest a clear set of decisions that leaders need to make in order to foster the business model's overall strength."[103]

---

[101] Verne Harnish, *Scaling Up*, 195.
[102] *David La Piana, The Nonprofit Strategy Revolution: Real-Time Strategic Planning in a Rapid-Response World,* New York: Fieldstone Alliance, 2008), 87.
[103] Bell, Masaoka, and Zimmerman, *Nonprofit Sustainability*, 25.

SCALING UP: People, Strategy, Execution, Cash

#1. People: Key Question: Are the stakeholders (staff, volunteers, campers, customers, board members) happy and engaged in the camp and would you "rehire" them?

#2. Strategy: Is our strategy providing sustaining revenues and desired mission impact? Does what we are planning to do really matter enough to our customers/constituents?

TOOL: BUSINESS MODEL TABLE

	Current Business Model			Future Business Model	
SCOPE	INCLUDES	DOES NOT INCLUDE		INCLUDES	DOES NOT INCLUDE
Geographic service area					
Customers served					
Programs/ Services Offered					
Funding Sources					

#3. Execution: Are all processes running without drama and driving financial sustainability and mission impact?

4 Execution Tools

- ☐ TOOL A: Market Analysis
- ☐ TOOL B: Trend Analysis
- ☐ TOOL C: Current Programs Review
- ☐ TOOL D: Future Program Evaluation

#4. Cash: Are systems in place so we won't run out of cash?

☑ CHECKLIST: The Board's Role in Ensuring Sustainability	True/ False	How does the board know?
Informed by our organization's revenue stream data and benchmark statistics the board initiates strategic goals for the organization. (See Murdock Trust tables in the Appendix.)		
Our current business model is sustainable.		
Systems are in place so that we won't run out of cash.		
Our organization is managing any short-term or long-term debt.		
We have operating reserves and are taking appropriate action to further build the reserves.		
The board is asking the right questions.		
Other:		

❏ TOOL A: MARKET ANALYSIS

RESOURCE	OUR STRENGTHS	OTHER CAMP'S STRENGTHS			HOW WE COMPARE?
	OUR CAMP	CAMP #1	CAMP #2	CAMP #3	
Campers (numbers, satisfaction, retention…)					
Rental Groups (numbers, satisfaction, retention…)					
Human Resources (staff, board, volunteers…)					
Funding (diversity, activities…)					
Programs (types, quality…)					
Mission Impact					

Session 14 ◆ The Board's Financial/Fiduciary Role: Long-Term Sustainability

❏ TOOL B: TREND ANALYSIS

TYPES OF TRENDS	DIRECTION OF TREND	COMMENTS
Need or demands for our programs	Needs or demands are __ Increasing __ Decreasing __ Staying about the same	
Need or demands for rentals	Needs or demands are __ Increasing __ Decreasing __ Staying about the same	
Available funding	Needs or demands are __ Increasing __ Decreasing __ Staying about the same	
Other Trends:		

"DON'T READ THIS BOOK!"[104]

"Let's consider briefly the relationship between obedience and strategic planning and the temptation to take control. When we follow the common path, we take control, trust ourselves to provide, and enact strategies to try to make things happen. We come up with our own big, hairy, audacious targets and expect God to bless and fund them. However,
**just because a goal is so big
it can only be accomplished if God shows up
does not mean it aligns with His will."**

Gary Hoag, R. Scott Rodin, Wes Willmer

---

[104] Gary G. Hoag, R. Scott Rodin, and Wesley K. Willmer, *The Choice: The Christ-Centered Pursuit of Kingdom Outcomes* (Winchester, VA: ECFAPress, 2014), 31. (See also "Don't Read This Book!" – A review of The Choice, by John Pearson, *John Pearson's Buckets Blog*, April 12, 2015, https://urgentink.typepad.com/my_weblog/2014/04/the-choice.html.)

Session 14 ◆ The Board's Financial/Fiduciary Role: Long-Term Sustainability

❑ TOOL C: CURRENT PROGRAMS REVIEW

Strategic Program Development Standard[105]
ANNUAL EVALUATION OF CURRENT AND FUTURE PROGRAMS
Primary Programs and Secondary Programs

☑ **FEED YOUR STRONGEST PROGRAMS AND BENCHMARK THE OTHERS**
ALL PROGRAMS ARE NOT CREATED EQUAL

PROGRAM STANDARD: Rate each program on a scale of 1 to 5 for each standard:	Program A	Program B	Program C	Program D	Program E
5 = Currently meets or exceeds standard 4 = Has met or exceeded standard at least 2 out of the last 3 years. 3 = Has not met the standard—but we agree it will likely meet it in the next year. 2 = No reason to believe it will meet the standard. 1 = Based on this standard, it is time to drop this program.					
☑ Program serves a minimum of ___% of our customers (members, donors, etc.)					
☑ Program generates a net income of ___%.					
☑ The measurable results of this program are improving each year.					
☑ Customer research and feedback indicate this program has strong appeal and/or potential.					
ADD ADDITIONAL STANDARDS HERE:					
TOTAL SCORES:					

Determine score ranges for primary programs and secondary programs.
(Example: Primary programs must score at least 37 out of 50 points.)

---

[105] John Pearson, *Mastering the Management Buckets*, 98.

Session 14 ◆ The Board's Financial/Fiduciary Role: Long-Term Sustainability

❏ TOOL D: FUTURE PROGRAM EVALUATION:

Top-10 Questions to Ask About Program Capacity and Sustainability[106]

☑ CHECK THE THREE MOST IMPORTANT FOR YOUR ORGANIZATION:

❏ 1. Does this program align with our mission statement?

❏ 2. Does this program align with our Big Holy Audacious Goal (BHAG)?

❏ 3. Does this program have written goals that meet the S.M.A.R.T. test (Specific, Measurable, Achievable, Realistic, Time-related)?

❏ 4. Do we have the people capacity to both launch the program and maintain it (a staff champion, support staff, volunteers, etc.)?

❏ 5. Have we answered the five Drucker questions?

❏ 6. Have we invested adequate time and money in researching *Who is the customer?* and *What does the customer value?*

❏ 7. Does this program align with our culture and our core values?

❏ 8. Have we conducted due diligence to assess the program's sustainability (including revenue and expense) over the next three to five years?

❏ 9. Under what conditions do we agree that we will "pull the plug" on this program if the goals are not achieved by the target dates?

❏ 10. Have we been diligent in asking our inside circle for constructive criticism or have we spiritually hyped it so much that naysayers have been silenced?

---

[106] John Pearson, *Mastering the Management Buckets Workbook: Management Tools, Templates, and Tips from John Pearson – Commentary by Jason Pearson*, 2nd ed. (San Clemente, CA: Pearpod, 2018), 68.

Session 14 ♦ The Board's Financial/Fiduciary Role: Long-Term Sustainability

❑ **7. HOMEWORK: THE MATRIX MAP -** Note! This was your "homework exercise" from Session 9. **Purpose:** Learn how to create a matrix map for your organization. Once completed, this will provide insights for making strategic decisions for financial viability. (Worksheets #4-9)

An Important Component of Your Strategic Planning Process

THE MATRIX MAP PROCESS
From: *Nonprofit Sustainability: Making Strategic Decisions for Financial Viability*[107]

High Mission Impact Low Profitability/Sustainability 	High Mission Impact High Profitability/Sustainability 
Low Mission Impact Low Profitability/Sustainability 	Low Mission Impact High Profitability/Sustainability 

The matrix map can be completed at one of three basic levels of complexity. Using <u>one</u> of the following methods, complete a Matrix Map for your organization on Worksheet #8.

❑ **Option #1: QUICK.** Use your best off-the-top-of-your-head guesstimating as to the cost and impact of each activity as you enter them into the matrix map (Worksheet #8).

❑ **Option #2: BETTER.** A more quantitative and balances approach—use data from your annual report and end of year financial statements to help you complete Worksheets #4-7. Use numbers to provide the data to enter into the matrix map.

❑ **Option #3: BEST.** An even more precise and granular analysis can be achieved using the full strategies from the book, *Nonprofit Sustainability: Making Strategic Decisions for Financial Viability*. Follow the book's direction to provide the numbers needed to complete the matrix map.

---

[107] Jeanne Bell, Jan Masaoka and Steve Zimmerman, *Nonprofit Sustainability: Making Strategic Decisions for Financial Viability* (San Francisco: Jossey-Bass, 2010), 25.

Session 14 ◆ The Board's Financial/Fiduciary Role: Long-Term Sustainability

THE MATRIX MAP PROCESS:

WORKSHEET #4: PROFITABILITY STATEMENT: Generate a highly generalized/ball park annual profitability statement for your organization. Make your best rough guess for both the income generated and the cost of each business activity (programs/services and fundraising efforts). Then calculate profit or loss for each activity.

PROGRAMS/SERVICES	INCOME (EARNED)	EXPENSES	PROFIT OR LOSS
FUNDRAISING	(CONTRIBUTED)		
Total			

Session 14 ◆ The Board's Financial/Fiduciary Role: Long-Term Sustainability

THE MATRIX MAP PROCESS:
WORKSHEET #5: CRITERIA FOR DETERMINING IMPACT: Generate a list of potential criteria for determining program impact and then select four criteria that would best fit your organization.

CRITERIA	☑ TOP 4 CHOICES

WORKSHEET #6: IMPACT ASSESSMENT: List your programs in the table below and the criteria you selected to evaluate impact in the top row. Then using the four criteria just selected, rate each of these activities for impact using the following scale:
    1…..Not much impact
    2…..Some impact
    3…..Very strong impact
    4…..Exceptional impact

PROGRAMS	Criteria #1: _____	Criteria #2: _____	Criteria #3: _____	Criteria #4: _____	Average Impact Score

Session 14 ◆ The Board's Financial/Fiduciary Role: Long-Term Sustainability

THE MATRIX MAP PROCESS:

WORKSHEET #7: PROFITABILITY AND IMPACT SCORING: Transfer the information from the Profitability Statement table, listing each of your organization's business activities along with the respective profit or loss amount and expense. Transfer the Average Impact Score for each activity from the Impact Assessment table to the table below.

BUSINESS ACTIVITY	Expense	Profit or Loss	Mission Impact

IMPACT/PROFITABILITY QUADRANTS: Adjust the Profitability Scale to fit your financial size and the Impact Scale to fit your impact numbers, as shown in the example below.[108]

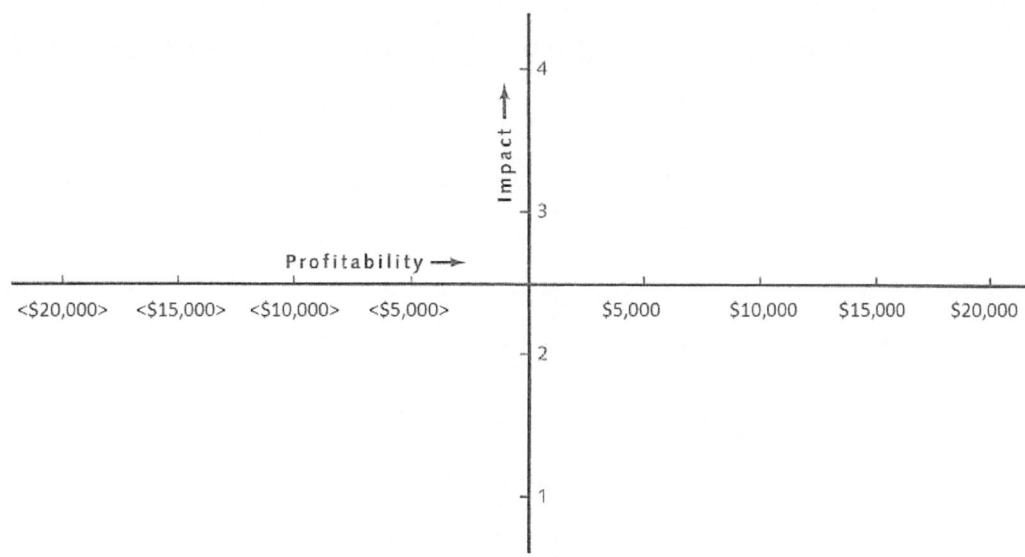

---

[108] Adapted from: *Nonprofit Sustainability*, Chapter 6, "Mapping the Matrix," 55-72.

THE MATRIX MAP PROCESS:

WORKSHEET #8: **FILL IN THE MATRIX MAP:** Plot your business activities in the appropriate quadrants. Use a different shape or color for fundraising activities than you do for program/services. You can roughly adjust the relative size of your shapes to correspond to the relative annual expenses of each activity.[109]

High Mission Impact Low Profitability/Sustainability	High Mission Impact High Profitability/Sustainability
Low Mission Impact Low Profitability/Sustainability	Low Mission Impact High Profitability/Sustainability

---

[109] Bell, Masaoka, Zimmerman, *Nonprofit Sustainability*, 58.

Session 14 ◆ The Board's Financial/Fiduciary Role: Long-Term Sustainability

THE MATRIX MAP PROCESS:

WORKSHEET #9: DECISION MAKING - STRATEGIC IMPERATIVES: Determine the Logic Imperatives indicated by your Matrix Map (to be completed at the Spring Session):

Use the data from your completed Matrix Map to populate the table below.

ACTIVITY	IMPACT	PROFIT	EFFORT	QUADRANT	ACTION

Session 14 ◆ The Board's Financial/Fiduciary Role: Long-Term Sustainability

❑ 8. PRESENTATION: *SCALING UP* (15 MINUTES INCLUDING Q & A)

Presenter	
Scaling Up Chapter	7. THE 7 STRATA OF STRATEGY: The Framework for Dominating Your Industry
#1. The big idea for our staff is:	
#2. The big idea for our board is:	
#3. I'm guessing that your biggest question about this chapter is:	

SCALING UP:
How a Few Companies Make It...and Why the Rest Don't
Mastering the Rockefeller Habits 2.0
by Verne Harnish

SCALING UP: THE 7 STRATA OF STRATEGY: The Framework for Dominating Your Industry **(pages 107-122)** [110]

NO.	THE 7 STRATA OF STRATEGY	NOTES
1	Words You Own (Mindshare)	
2	Sandbox and Brand Promises	
3	Brand Promise Guarantee (Catalytic Mechanism)	
4	One-PHRASE Strategy (Key to Making Money)	
5	Differentiating Activities (3 to 5 How's)	
6	X-Factor (10x-100x Underlying Advantage)	
7	Profit per X (Economic Engine) and BHAG® (10- to 25-Year Goal)	

---

[110] Verne Harnish, *Scaling Up*, 107-122.

SESSION 15

Strategic Tools and Templates for… Board Best Practices and Sustainability

SESSION 15:
Strategic Tools and Templates for Board Best Practices and Sustainability

☑ HEALTHY GOVERNANCE CHECKLIST
CCCA Thriving Boards ◆ Growing Healthy, Effective Boards

#15. THE BOARD APPROVES A SHORT LIST OF TOOLS AND TEMPLATES THAT WILL ENHANCE TRUST, INFORMATION FLOW, AND EFFECTIVE GOVERNANCE.
- ❏ The board affirms the standard format of agendas, written reports, recommendations, and minutes for all board meetings (including before, during, and after board meetings).
- ❏ The board affirms the standard format and frequency of CEO written reports—between board meetings.
- ❏ The board affirms the frequency and deadlines of all reports (example: seven days before a board meeting…).
- ❏ At least annually, the CEO and board chair review the effectiveness of the current tools and templates and, if needed, recommend changes to the board.

IN THIS SESSION:

❏ 1. <u>Discussion</u>: Why Are Tools and Templates So Important?

❏ 2. <u>Breakout With Coaches</u>: Guidance in Picking 3 to 5 Tools You Can Start Using This Month!

"If you want to teach people a new way of thinking, don't bother trying to teach them. Instead, **give them a tool,** the use of which will lead to new ways of thinking."[111]

R. Buckminster Fuller, *Designer, Inventor, Futurist*

"At least once
every five years,
every form
should be put on trial for its life."[112]

Peter Drucker, *the father of modern management*

---

[111] Verne Harnish, *Scaling Up*, 1.
[112] Peter F. Drucker, *The Practice of Management* (New York: HarperBusiness, 2006), 135.

Session 15 ◆ Strategic Tools and Templates for Board Best Practices and Sustainability

❏ 1. DISCUSSION: WHY ARE TOOLS AND TEMPLATES SO IMPORTANT?
Leverage the right tool or template to enrich board effectiveness and create a climate of trust and candor.

Don't Dump on Directors the Night Before!
TRUST CAN BE BROKEN AT ANY POINT

Why are tools and templates so important? "A virtuous cycle of respect, trust, and candor can be broken at any point."[113]

According to Jeffrey Sonnenfeld, building an effective board involves at least five critical elements:

- ☑ Creating a climate of trust and candor
- ☑ Fostering a culture of open dissent
- ☑ Utilizing a fluid portfolio of roles
- ☑ Ensuring individual accountability
- ☑ Evaluating the board's performance

He adds, "A virtuous cycle of respect, trust, and candor can be broken at any point. One of the most common breaks occurs when the CEO doesn't trust the board enough to share information.

"What kind of CEO waits until the night before the board meeting to dump on the directors a phone-book size report that includes, buried in a thicket of sub clauses and footnotes, the news that earnings are off for the second consecutive quarter? Surely not a CEO who trusts his or her board."[114]

With the right tools and templates, board chairs and CEOs will build and enhance trust.

Peter Drucker

TOOL COMPETENCE

"Although I don't know a single for-profit business that is as well managed as a few of the nonprofits, the great majority of the nonprofits can be graded a 'C' at best. Not for lack of effort; most of them work very hard. But for lack of focus, and for lack of tool competence."[115]

---

[113] Jeffrey A. Sonnenfeld, "What Makes Great Boards Great," *Harvard Business Review*, September 2002.
[114] Ibid.
[115] Peter F. Drucker, Frances Hesselbein, and Joan Snyder Kuhl, *Peter Drucker's Five Most Important Questions*, 2.

Session 15 ◆ Strategic Tools and Templates for Board Best Practices and Sustainability

TOOLS AND TEMPLATES WILL ENHANCE BOARDROOM TRUST...
...if you build your trust with these two principles in mind:

❏ PRINCIPLE NO. 1: THE FAITH-BASED FOUNDATION

The recommended resource, *ECFA Tools and Templates for Effective Board Governance*, is built on a foundation of Christ-centered governance. These tools have been tested hundreds of times in faith-based nonprofit organizations. As David McKenna wisely notes in *Call of the Chair*, **"A major difference between Christ-centered ministries and for-profit or nonprofit organizations is in the question, 'Who gets the credit?'"**[116]

Certainly nonprofit boards of all types will find value in these tools and templates, but those who serve in Christ-centered organizations will understand the language, our lexicon—and our motivation.

❏ PRINCIPLE NO. 2: LEVERAGE FOR IMPACT!

If you knew that by leveraging a specific tool or template it would exponentially enhance your communication, your outcomes, your results, and your governance joy—you'd do it right? Then heed this simple, but powerful premise from Dan Busby: "Christ-centered ministries with…

- ✓ Trusted Governance,
- ✓ Trusted Resource-raising, and
- ✓ Trusted Resource Management…

…experience elevated Kingdom outcomes."[117]

When leaders and board members leverage the right tools and templates—*at the right time and for the right reasons*—they will build trust. And trust will pave the way for God-honoring results.

Example: CEOs and senior pastors have told us that by using the "5/15 Monthly Report to the Board" template, they have enhanced communication—and trust—with their board members. One CEO even called the template a "home run."[118]

We also encourage you to read *Lessons From the Nonprofit Boardroom* (*Second Edition, 2018*) as a companion resource to *ECFA Tools and Templates for Effective Board Governance*. You'll find additional color commentary on several tools and templates including the "Board Policies Manual," "Ten Minutes for Governance," and the "CEO's 5/15 Monthly Report to the Board."

---

[116] David L. McKenna, *Call of the Chair: Leading the Board of the Christ-Centered Ministry* (Winchester, VA: ECFAPress, 2017), 93.
[117] Dan Busby, *Trust*, 2.
[118] Busby and Pearson, *Lessons From the Nonprofit Boardroom*, 29.

Session 15 ◆ Strategic Tools and Templates for Board Best Practices and Sustainability

❏ **2. BREAKOUT WITH COACHES:**
GUIDANCE IN PICKING 3 TO 5 TOOLS YOU CAN START USING THIS MONTH!

TOOLS AND TEMPLATES

PRIORITY: A B C	TOOLS AND TEMPLATES ☑ = Top-5 Tools to begin using this month	TARGET DATE	POINT PERSON
	❏ Tool #1: The Pathway to the Board		
	❏ Tool #2: Board Nominee Suggestion Form		
	❏ Tool #3: Board Nominee Orientation: Table of Contents		
	❏ Tool #4: Five-Finger Feedback		
	❏ Tool #5: Board's Annual Self-Assessment Survey		
	❏ Tool #6: The Board's Annual Financial Management Audit		
	❏ Tool #7: The Board's Annual Legal Audit		
	❏ Tool #8: The Board's Annual Fundraising Audit		
	❏ Tool #9: The Board's Annual Evaluation of the Top Leader		
	❏ Tool #10: The 5/15 Monthly Report to the Board		
	❏ Tool #11: Monthly Dashboard Report		
	❏ Tool #12: Quarterly Board Meeting Agenda & Recommendations		
	❏ Tool #13: Board Retreat Read-and-Reflect Worksheets		
	❏ Tool #14: The Rolling 3-Year Strategic Plan Placemat		
	❏ Tool #15: Board Retreat Trend-Spotting Exercise		
	❏ Tool #16: Prime Responsibility Chart		
	❏ Tool #17: Board Policies Manual (BPM)		
	❏ Tool #18: Job Descriptions for the Top Leader and Board Chair		
	❏ Tool #19: Ten Minutes for Governance		
	❏ Tool #20: Tent Cards and Tools for Leveraging Board Strengths		
	❏ Tool #21: Board Member Annual Affirmation Statement		
	❏ Tool #22: Straw Vote Cards		

➔**Reminder!** If you, or your organization, purchased this book (or received it as part of a board training/enrichment experience), you are authorized to download the templates. (See the templates webpage and password on the title page of the book.)

SESSION 16

The Evening Dessert Hour:

Continuing the Promise

SESSION 16:
The Evening Dessert Hour: Continuing the Promise

NOTES:

SESSION 17

Board Service: A Sacred Trust

SESSION 17:
Board Service: A Sacred Trust

IN THIS SESSION:

❑ 1. <u>Morning Insight</u>: Board Service—A Sacred Trust

❑ 2. <u>Around-the-Table</u>: A Board Prayer by Dan Bolin (read the prayer together from Session 7)

❏ 1. MORNING INSIGHT: BOARD SERVICE—A SACRED TRUST

Relationship Wisdom in the Boardroom[119]

Ed McDowell

"UNDERSTAND THIS, my dear brothers and sisters: You must all be…
✓ quick to listen,
✓ slow to speak, and
✓ slow to get angry."

James 1:19 *NLT*

Every person I have ever met or known wants to have healthy and meaningful relationships in their lives. Around the many campfires of Warm Beach Camp I have had the privilege of listening to the joy of people enjoying good relationships and the pain of broken families, marriages and friendships. There is a common thread in all of it: People long for good relationships in their lives.

Good relationships have some things in common. Here are three points of wisdom from the Bible for anyone interested in cultivating healthy relationships in every sector of our lives:

▶ **1. Be quick to listen.** Listening is the core activity in understanding where someone else is coming from. We live in a culture where "quick to speak" is the norm. Talking all the time gives no room to understand someone else. Constant talking becomes me-centric. Listening is the foundation for knowing other people.

▶ **2. Slow to speak.** It has been said that true listening is not thinking about the next thing to be said as soon as there is a break in the conversation. Listening is receiving what the other person has to say, and actually reflecting on it. Ask clarifying questions about their content to encourage further understanding. Resist trying to get the next word in.

▶ **3. Slow to get angry.** Anger in relationships does not produce good results. Hot-tempered, quick-flashing anger creates incredible instability in other people. Trust and safety are eroded. There are appropriate uses of anger, but it is far less often than we might think. Don't get angry over the insignificant. Don't come to anger quickly. Reserve anger as a response to significant issues of relationship that are not right. Even then, be very slow and careful in showing anger in a way that communicates true concern because this relationship really matters.

---

[119] Ed McDowell, "Relationship Wisdom in the Boardroom" –unpublished blog/book chapter, © Copyright 2019, Ed McDowell. All rights reserved - *https://www.standpoint360.com*

Session 17 ◆ Board Service: A Sacred Trust

> Consider increasing your ability to listen to others. Focus less on what you are going to say. Only use anger in a thoughtful and measured way that communicates true concern for the relationship on important issues.
>
> God's word comes through again, giving us wisdom for all of our relationships.

NOTES:

❑ 2. AROUND-THE-TABLE: A BOARD PRAYER BY DAN BOLIN
(Read the prayer together from Session 7.)

My Prayer:

SESSION 18

The Board's Role in Owning the *Assumptions*...

...That Undergird Our Business Model and Strategic Plan

SESSION 18:
The Board's Role in Owning the *Assumptions* That Undergird Our Business Model and Strategic Plan

> ☑ **HEALTHY GOVERNANCE CHECKLIST**
> CCCA Thriving Boards ◆ Growing Healthy, Effective Boards
>
> **#18. THE BOARD OWNS THE ASSUMPTIONS THAT UNDERGIRD THE BUSINESS MODEL AND THE STRATEGIC PLAN.**
> ❑ Board members engage in a staff/board/stakeholder planning process that includes the consideration of numerous assumptions—culminating in a thoughtful list of "Our Top-10 Assumptions for 20___."
> ❑ The board affirms the annual written document, "Our Top-10 Assumptions for 20___."
> ❑ Every board member engages regularly with key volunteers, donors, primary customers, supporting customers, and others to solicit feedback on "Our Top-10 Assumptions for 20___."
> ❑ Board members ensure that there is alignment between the Top-10 Assumptions and the business model and strategic plan—and prayer and discernment undergirds this year-round feedback process.

IN THIS SESSION:

❑ 1. <u>Round-the-Room</u>: Our Strategic Planning Process (and Model)

❑ 2. <u>Read</u>: Lesson 39: Identify Your Key Assumptions (from *More Lessons From the Nonprofit Boardroom*)

❑ 3. <u>Exercise</u>: The Radar Report: Help! What Are You Seeing Out There?

❑ 4. <u>Presentation</u>: *Scaling Up*: "15 Minutes Including Q & A" – "The One Page Strategic Plan"

❑ 5. <u>Presentation</u>: *Scaling Up*: "15 Minutes Including Q & A" – (presenter's choice!)

Book: *United Breaks Guitars*[120]

Video: *United Breaks Guitars*[121]

---

[120] Dave Carroll, *United Breaks Guitars: The Power of One Voice in the Age of Social Media* (Carlsbad, CA: Hay House, 2012).
[121] The viral video, "United Breaks Guitars," is noted in *Team of Teams: New Rules of Engagement for a Complex World*, by Gen. Stanley McChrystal with Tantum Collins, David Silverman, and Chris Fussell. (Read John Pearson's review at: http://urgentink.typepad.com/my_weblog/2016/06/team-of-teams.html.)

Session 18 ◆ The Board's Role in Owning the Assumptions

❑ 1. ROUND-THE-ROOM: OUR STRATEGIC PLANNING PROCESS (AND MODEL)

REMINDER: *This is a year-long program in effective governance, NOT strategic planning! So the big question here is: "What is the <u>board's role</u> in owning <u>the strategy</u> and the <u>assumptions</u> undergirding our business model and strategic plan?"*

NOTES ON BEST PRACTICES:

ORGANIZATIONS	STRATEGIC PLANNING BEST PRACTICES AND METHODOLOGIES

☑ **One Big Idea for Our Organization:**

Session 18 ◆ The Board's Role in Owning the Assumptions

❑ 2. READ: LESSON 39: IDENTIFY YOUR KEY ASSUMPTIONS

LESSON 39: IDENTIFY YOUR KEY ASSUMPTIONS[122]
An inaccurate premise may lead to a colossal flop!

From: **More Lessons From the Nonprofit Boardroom: Effectiveness, Excellence, Elephants**! by Dan Busby and John Pearson

Reprinted by permission of ECFAPress.

> *Meetings are a good place to discover whether an organization might be suffering from groupthink. If everyone in the room seems convinced of the brilliance of an idea, it may be a sign that the organization would benefit from more dissent and debate.*[123]
>
> Donald Rumsfeld

The silence was deafening. Board members gulped. Their red-in-the-face CEO had just delivered the shocking news. The *Vision 100 Challenge*—unanimously and enthusiastically affirmed by the board—had flopped.

Three major donors, and a generous foundation, had shared the ministry's enthusiasm for this out-of-the-box initiative. The largest donations in the organization's history were the sent-from-heaven lead gifts that fueled a robust fundraising campaign. *For the first time ever—lack of funds was not the problem.*

But there was a problem. The program—an enormously costly venture—had failed miserably.

> *Remember the story of the dog food company's annual sales meeting—when the VP of sales castigated her regional sales reps for declining sales? The executive harangued the discouraged sales agents: "What's going on here? We have the greatest ad campaigns. Our packaging is award-winning. We've improved distribution. So...why are our dog food sales so dismal?"*
>
> *An anonymous voice from the back of the room answered,* **"The dogs don't like it!"**

Good news. There is help for dog food purveyors and ministry board members. At your next board meeting—ask this simple question:

"What are our assumptions about the _____?"

Just fill in the blanks with your current opportunity, project, or plan (strategic plan, annual plan, ABC Vision Initiative, XYZ Challenge, etc.).

---

[122] Busby and Pearson, *More Lessons From the Nonprofit Boardroom* (See Lesson 39.)
[123] Donald Rumsfeld, *Rumsfeld's Rules: Leadership Lessons in Business, Politics, War, and Life* (New York: HarperCollins Publishers, 2013), 39.

Session 18 ◆ The Board's Role in Owning the Assumptions

Assumptions are a very big deal—and had the ministry above invested adequate time in identifying their key assumptions about the *Vision 100 Challenge,* they likely could have prevented an embarrassing flop and an egregious waste of God's money.

In the chapter "Thinking Strategically," in *Rumsfeld's Rules: Leadership Lessons in Business, Politics, War, and Life*, Donald Rumsfeld lists four critical strategic planning steps:[124]
- Step 1: Set the Goals
- Step 2: **Identify Your Key Assumptions**
- Step 3: Determine the Best Course of Action
- Step 4: Monitor Progress Through Metrics

Rumsfeld writes that the second step "tends to be one of the most neglected. Assumptions are often left unstated, it being taken for granted that everyone around a table knows what they are, when frequently that is not the case. The assumptions that are hidden or held subconsciously are the ones that often get you into trouble." (Think dog food—will the *dogs* like it?) He adds:

> **"It is possible to proceed perfectly logically from an inaccurate premise to an inaccurate and unfortunate conclusion."**[125]

Rumsfeld, who was U.S. Secretary of Defense twice (and a Fortune 500 CEO twice), describes a planning meeting at the Pentagon: "The objective of the plan was straightforward enough: to defend South Korean sovereignty and defeat the North Korean threat. What I found troubling, however, was that there was no discussion of the key assumptions in which the plan was rooted."

Rumsfeld dismissed the meeting and they reconvened on the next Saturday. "That Saturday we met for hours and never discussed any of the plans, only the assumptions."[126]

Are you willing to risk your ministry's future—with inadequate premises that lead to unfortunate conclusions? We recommend you identify your "Top-10 Assumptions" that you believe are foundational to your programs, products, and services. Here are some examples:

☑ **A RESCUE MISSION.** A social services ministry in a major city noted a trend that many of their homeless guests had previously lived in three nearby suburbs. **Assumption:** *If we create partnerships with key churches in key suburbs—and provide church leaders and volunteers with training and know-how—perhaps those churches could minister to local people in need before they are at a crisis point in their lives.*

☑ **A COLLEGE.** The growing backlash against high tuition costs at private colleges (and even the need for a higher education) may endanger the very existence of our Christian college. **Assumption:** *Within X years, student debt for graduating seniors must equate more to car loan levels versus home mortgage levels.*

☑ **A FOUNDER-LED MISSION.** The aging donor base—hundreds and hundreds of faithful friends of the founder—will soon dry up (and die). **Assumption:** *Our future depends on our*

---
[124] Ibid., 68-88.
[125] Ibid., 76.
[126] Ibid., 77-78.

ability to inspire the children and grandchildren of our current donors to take the giving baton—before our founder retires (or dies).

☑ **A MEDIA MINISTRY.** The trends away from traditional TV and radio programming—toward podcasts and streaming—are the hot topics at our industry gatherings. **Assumption:** *We must break out of our traditional ministry model bubble (talking to ourselves, working harder—not smarter, etc.) and probably double our research budget immediately—so we're not caught flat-footed in a changing technological environment.*

Many boards and senior teams have intentional, robust discussions about "assumptions"—culminating in a one-page document (some call it their "Radar Report"). Then, board members, the CEO, and senior team members look for opportunities to review that one-page report with stakeholders and trend-spotters—asking for informal feedback, like this:

> "Mary, thanks for meeting with us today. In addition to talking about our capital campaign—would you look over this one-page list of 'Our Top-10 Assumptions: The Radar Report' right now? Are these the right assumptions? What's missing? What would you add or delete?"

We urge board members to be receptive to the Lord's "Tap! Tap! Tap!" on the shoulders of their hearts—not just at board meetings, but 24/7—every day.[127] Listen for the Holy Spirit's nudge—every day—and look for opportunities to discuss these assumptions with a colleague or even an acquaintance that is not familiar with your ministry. Perhaps God will plant just the right person in your path so your inaccurate assumptions don't lead to inaccurate conclusions—or a colossal flop!

There are many reasons why you should ask volunteers, donors, and others for feedback. R. Mark Dillon notes that "big ideas attract big gifts." He urges CEOs, pastors, and fundraisers to engage givers at the front end of a project. "Big ideas are mission-centered." He quotes one gifted giver, "Please don't come to me with an 'order list' already thought out, where my only decision is how much to give!"

Dillon notes, "When the organization has done all the thinking and only wants capital from the giver, they have forfeited not only wise counsel but also a deeper relationship and, most probably the big gift as well."[128]

Rumsfeld would agree with Dillon. Here's a Rumsfeld rule that is worth memorizing:

"If you expect people to be in on the landing, include them for the takeoff."

---

[127] Read Steve Macchia's convicting insights in Lesson 11, "Tap! Tap! Tap!" in *Lessons From the Nonprofit Boardroom*, by Dan Busby and John Pearson.
[128] R. Mark Dillon, *Giving and Getting in the Kingdom: A Field Guide* (Chicago: Moody Publishers, 2012), 65.

Session 18 ◆ The Board's Role in Owning the Assumptions

In addition to insights on assumptions—a neglected key component for stewarding your resources and preventing flops—you'll enjoy reading and repeating many of Rumsfeld's 400 rules, including:

- "The first consideration for meetings is whether to call one at all."
- "If you can find something everyone agrees on, it's wrong." (Rep. Mo Udall)
- "The default tendency in any bureaucracy, especially in government, is to substitute discussion for decision-making. The act of calling a meeting about a problem can in some cases be confused with actually doing something."
- "Stubborn opposition to proposals often has no basis other than the complaining question, 'Why wasn't I consulted?'" (Pat Moynihan)
- "If you don't know what your top three priorities are, you don't have priorities."
- "What you measure improves."[129]

We end with this caution about fake news! Peter Drucker, often called "the world's greatest management thinker," famously said, "What everyone knows is usually wrong." William Cohen's book, *The Practical Drucker,"* notes:

> What Drucker wanted to emphasize was that we must always question our assumptions, no matter from where they originate. This is especially so regarding anything that a majority of people "know" or assume without questioning. This "knowledge" should always be suspect and needs to be examined closer because, in a surprisingly high percentage of cases, the information "known to be true" will turn out to be inaccurate or completely false. This can lead to extremely poor, even disastrous management decisions.[130]

BOARDROOM LESSON
Identify your key assumptions so your inaccurate premises don't lead to inaccurate conclusions and colossal flops! Invest time in assessing the validity of your assumptions—and asking for advice and counsel from others. Expect God to lead you to colleagues, acquaintances, and even experts who will give you feedback on your ministry's important plans and your assumptions about those plans.

Board Action Steps:

❏ **1. Allocate:** Begin your process by allocating 30 minutes at your next board meeting to discuss assumptions. Ask board members and senior team members to read this lesson in advance—and then in groups of two or three—ask each group to identify their key assumptions (up to 10).

---

[129] Donald Rumsfeld, *Rumsfeld's Rules*, 299-331. (Note: Appendix B includes the master list of 400 Rumsfeld's Rules. The book includes color commentaries on dozens of the Rumsfeld's favorite rules.)
[130] William A. Cohen, *The Practical Drucker,* 55-56. (Read Chapter 9, "What Everyone Knows Is Usually Wrong.")

Session 18 ◆ The Board's Role in Owning the Assumptions

❍ **2. Assess:** Ask the CEO and senior team to combine and narrow down the lists of assumptions—and give the board the first draft of the one-page document, "Our Top-10 Assumptions: The Radar Report."

❍ **3. Advise:** After the board affirms or edits the first draft, then it's time to review the "Radar Report" with others. Be intentional about seeking the advice and counsel of colleagues, friends, acquaintances, experts, givers, volunteers, former board and staff members, and others. The feedback will sharpen your plan.

> *Prayer*
> "Lord, protect us from colossal flops!
> Give us humility as we seek the counsel and advice of others so that we follow Your plans. Guide us to the correct premises that will lead us to Kingdom impact for Your glory. Amen."

Session 18 ◆ The Board's Role in Owning the Assumptions

BONUS PAGE!

For more reading on assumptions:

The Mindset Lists of American History: From Typewriters to Text Messages—What Ten Generations of Americans Think Is Normal,
by Tom McBride and Ron Nief

Read John Pearson's review.[131]

THE MINDSET LIST: College Class of 2022
http://themindsetlist.com/

Visit "The Mindset List for the Class of 2022" (those who entered college in the fall of 2018) for a great example showing how college administrators and faculty view the Class of 2022. Here are a few of the 60 insights on the list:

- They are the first class born in the new millennium, escaping the dreaded label of "Millennial," though their new designation—iGen, GenZ, etc. — has not yet been agreed upon by them.
- Outer space has never been without human habitation.
- They have always been able to refer to Wikipedia.
- They have grown up afraid that a shooting could happen at their school, too.
- Calcutta has always been Kolkata.
- Afghanistan has always been the frustrating quagmire that keeps on giving.
- When filling out forms, they are not surprised to find more than two gender categories to choose from.
- Presidential candidates winning the popular vote and then losing the election are not unusual.
- Parents have always been watching *Big Brother*, and vice versa.
- They've grown up with stories about where their grandparents were on 11/22/63 and where their parents were on 9/11.
- They will never fly TWA, Swissair, or Sabena airlines.
- There has never been an Enron.
- The Prius has always been on the road in the U.S.
- They never used a spit bowl in a dentist's office.
- "You've got mail" would sound as ancient to them as "number, please" would have sounded to their parents.
- A visit to a bank has been a rare event.
- They have never had to deal with "chads," be they dimpled, hanging, or pregnant.
- Exotic animals have always been providing emotional support to passengers on planes.
- Robots have always been able to walk on two legs and climb stairs.
- Mass market books have always been available exclusively as Ebooks.
- Donny and Marie who?
- There have always been more than a billion people in India.

© Copyright 2018 Ron Nief.
Mindset List® is a registered trademark.

---

[131] John Pearson, "The Mindset Lists of American History", *John Pearson's Buckets Blog*, April 19, 2012, https://urgentink.typepad.com/my_weblog/2012/04/the-mindset-lists-of-american-history.html.

❏ **3. EXERCISE:**
THE RADAR REPORT: HELP! WHAT ARE YOU SEEING OUT THERE?

ASSUMPTIONS EXERCISE:

Instructions:
The *Radar Report* is a simple, no-cost way to keep research on the front burner. It involves four steps:

❏ **STEP 1: Identify up to 50 questions or assumptions about the future—and then slim the list down to your "Top-10 Assumptions."** You're asking yourself, "What's on the radar? What do we need to be watching for—so we are not blindsided by a threat or opportunity."

❏ **STEP 2: Solicit face-to-face feedback.** Carry copies of the *Radar Report* with you everywhere you go:
- Board meetings
- Vendor appointments
- One-on-one fundraising contacts
- Interviews with future volunteers and staff
- Your small group at church
- Meetings with industry/profession leaders, government officials, professors, etc.
- Ask these people to quickly review the *Radar Report* and give you feedback. Don't ask them to email it or mail it back—just get their immediate feedback. You will bless them for asking—and you'll gain amazing insights. Your assumptions will be confirmed or challenged.

❏ **STEP 3: Compile these opinions and keep a running total.** This is not a scientific survey, it's an opinion survey. But every once in a while, you will uncover a gem—and it could eventually become a major fork-in-the-road idea that informs your strategic planning process.

Extra Credit!

If you have time, recruit a volunteer to compile the results AND to send a hand-written thank you note to the *Radar Report* Responder. A hand-written thank you note? That will shock them! (Add a $5 Starbucks card—and they'll be your friend for life!)

Session 18 ◆ The Board's Role in Owning the Assumptions

ORGANIZATION NAME: _____

RADAR REPORT
Our Top-10 Assumptions: 2020

HELP! WHAT ARE YOU SEEING OUT THERE?

Every year, we create this one-page *Radar Report* to test the assumptions in the Environmental Scan section of our Rolling 3-Year Strategic Plan. If our assumptions are incorrect—or we're asking the wrong question—we'll likely get the wrong answers…and the domino effect kicks in. That's why we appreciate your help!

Are these the right questions and the right assumptions about the future for our organization?

No.	QUESTIONS AND ASSUMPTIONS ABOUT THE FUTURE	Is this the right question or assumption?
1		Yes No
2		Yes No
3		Yes No
4		Yes No
5		Yes No
6		Yes No
7		Yes No
8		Yes No
9		Yes No
10		Yes No

COMMENTS:

Name _____   Date _____

Email _____   Phone _____

191 | Thriving Boards Workbook ◆ 4th Edition

Session 18 ◆ The Board's Role in Owning the Assumptions

❑ 4. PRESENTATION:
SCALING UP: "15 MINUTES INCLUDING Q & A" – "THE ONE PAGE STRATEGIC PLAN"

Presenter	
Scaling Up Chapter	8. THE ONE-PAGE STRATEGIC PLAN: The Tool for Strategic Planning
#1. The big idea for our staff is:	
#2. The big idea for our board is:	
#3. I'm guessing that your biggest question about this chapter is:	

**SCALING UP:
How a Few Companies Make It…and Why the Rest Don't**
Mastering the Rockefeller Habits 2.0
by Verne Harnish

SCALING UP: 8. THE ONE-PAGE STRATEGIC PLAN: The Tool for Strategic Planning (pages 123-140) [132]

NO.	THE ONE-PAGE PLAN	NOTES
1	Column 1: Should/Shouldn't	
2	Column 2: Why	
3	Column 3: Where	
4	Column 4: What	
5	Column 5: How	
6	Column 6: Finish Lines and Fun	
7	Column 7: Who	

---

[132] Verne Harnish, *Scaling Up*, 107-122

Session 18 ◆ The Board's Role in Owning the Assumptions

❑ 5. PRESENTATION: *SCALING UP* (15 MINUTES INCLUDING Q & A)

Presenter	
Scaling Up Chapter	
#1. The big idea for our staff is:	
#2. The big idea for our board is:	
#3. I'm guessing that your biggest question about this chapter is:	

**SCALING UP:
How a Few Companies
Make It...and
Why the Rest Don't**
*Mastering the Rockefeller
Habits 2.0*
by Verne Harnish

SCALING UP: (pages _____) [133]

NO.	TOPICS	NOTES
1		
2		
3		
4		
5		
6		
7		

---

[133] Verne Harnish, *Scaling Up*.

SESSION 19

The Board's Role in Embracing the Donor

Part 2

Session 19 ◆ The Board's Role in Embracing the Donor (Part 2)

SESSION 19:
The Board's Role in Embracing the Donor (Part 2)

> ☑ **HEALTHY GOVERNANCE CHECKLIST**
> CCCA Thriving Boards ◆ Growing Healthy, Effective Boards
>
> **Note:** This checklist is repeated from Session 8.
> **#8. BOARD MEMBERS AFFIRM THEIR IMPORTANT ROLES WITH DONORS.**
> ❑ Board member recruitment and orientation includes expectations about generous giving.
> ❑ Board member recruitment and orientation includes affirmations about building relationships with others.
> ❑ Board members are coached and each board member's development role is customized according to a board member's 3 Powerful S's (Spiritual Gifts, Strengths, and Social Styles—see Session 5).
> ❑ Board members affirm and live out the ministry's written "Theology of Development."[134]

IN THIS SESSION:

❑ 1. <u>Reminders</u>: The Essentials of Development: It's All About the Heart

❑ 2. <u>Discuss</u>: Three Roles for the Board (Leadership, Advocacy, Involvement)

❑ 3. <u>Review</u>: Four Keys and Four Cautions!

❑ 4. <u>Table Work</u>: Individual and Group Questions

DEVELOPMENT 101 is unrivaled—literally nothing like it. It's detailed, but short enough that board members will read it. The 30,000-foot view is panoramic and motivating ("I could do this!") and the in-the-weeds details are amazing. Consultant-types don't give away the store in print. They did!

Example: "The Role of the Board in Development" (Chapter 3) has four keys and four cautions to help board members be successful development partners. "Review your Board Scope of Work (or whatever documents articulate your board policies and procedures) frequently at board meetings to reinforce the work everyone agreed to take on when they joined."

If you think you're beyond a "Development 101" title—don't! It's comprehensive as the subtitle promises, including: theological foundations, the key role of relationships, "Ten Components to Your Comprehensive Annual Development Plan," the strategic plan, volunteers, capital campaign strategies, planned giving, and three short pages/words-of-wisdom on how and why to hang in there.[135]

---

[134] John R. Frank and R. Scott Rodin, *Development 101*, 7-17. (See also "An Example of a Theology of Development" on pages 143-148.)

[135] From John Pearson's review of *Development 101* by Frank and Rodin. *"2 Books: Development 101 and Igniting Your Generosity,"* June 23, 2015, John Pearson's Buckets Blog (blog), https://urgentink.typepad.com/my_weblog/2015/06/2-books-development-101-and-igniting-your-generosity.html.

❑ 1. REMINDERS: THE ESSENTIALS OF DEVELOPMENT: IT'S ALL ABOUT THE HEART

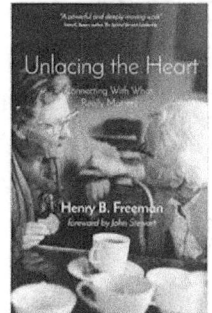

Fundraising is not the knowledge and skills we possess…

At its core it is not what we learn with our heads but a gift we receive with our hearts. It is the gift of being invited into another person's life; an invitation to be 'present' in a vulnerable space where our walls come down and our masks are taken off. A space where human beings connect and lives are transformed.[136]

3 REMINDERS:

❑ **Different Roles:**
- Board Members
- Executive Directors
- Donors (time, expertise, money, Gift-in-Kind)
- Development Team Member
- Quick Review of "Embrace of the Donor" Diagram (See session handout.)

❑ **Essentials of Development** - The backdrop for the donor romance:
- Prayer
- Case Statement
- Development Plan
- Segmented Donor List
- Development Team

❑ **All About the HEART:**
- Feeling the Heartbeat of the Organization
- Unlacing Hearts, Our Own and the Donors
- Development is all about relationship. God has hardwired us all to be in relationship.

---

[136] Henry B. Freeman, *Unlacing the Heart: Connecting With What Really Matters* (Richmond, IN: H. Freeman Associates, 2015), 90-91.

❏ 2. DISCUSS:
THREE ROLES FOR THE BOARD (LEADERSHIP, ADVOCACY, INVOLVEMENT)

Content for this session was adapted from Chapter 3, "The Role of the Board in Development," with some soft "fluff" added by Nancy Nelson! Used by permission.[137]

Development 101: Building a Comprehensive Development Program on Biblical Values
by John R. Frank and R. Scott Rodin

☑ ROLE NO. 1: LEADERSHIP

THE 4 P'S

Prayer	Soak the gathering of resources in prayer. If we are wanting fruit for the Kingdom, we must be connected to the Vine.
Passion	There is nothing more incredibly attractive and wooing to prospective donors (be they volunteers, GIK or cash donors) than passion for the Kingdom mission. "The fire in the belly!" Sometimes it needs to be ignited. And, like fire, passion is contagious.
Perspective	It is entirely possible to do the steps in embracing the donor and have it nothing more than "moves management," just using relationships as a means to an end. When you are just checking off the boxes, this can turn out to be nothing more than a process of manipulation. Giving for the donor turns out to be transactional, not transformational. The heart of the donor has not been touched. Their heart has not been unlaced to feel the heartbeat of the ministry. **Looking through the lens that sees Development as ministry.** We are all on a journey of becoming faithful stewards where God is developing in us a heart of a faithful stewards. **Create a sacred space.** In order to connect donors to the heartbeat of the ministry, we must first become vulnerable and unlace our own hearts and then help the donor to do the same if they are going to feel the joy in becoming better stewards of what God has entrusted them with. It's creating a "sacred space" between two people.

---
[137] Frank and Rodin, *Development 101*, 27-42.

Session 19 ◆ The Board's Role in Embracing the Donor (Part 2)

	According to a seasoned fundraising consultant, Henry Freeman, in *Unlacing the Heart,* we must have passion for a cause and be willing to share the dream, but not a dream that is just mine and I ask the prospective donor to support.[138] We need to find others who share the same dream and give ownership away. We are not looking for donors, but "partners." All of the other things acquired to do this embracing of the donor are simply vehicles or tools that help unlace the heart. Freeman also has learned to see the vulnerable person that resides in each of us. It's in the sacred space we all seek, a place where we feel welcomed and at home. We are all broken human beings and on a journey to become better stewards of what God has entrusted us with, including our time, talents and finances. In the process, we all become more whole as human beings. Remember that God has hardwired us to be involved in something bigger than ourselves. We become more whole when we get connected to that purpose. Fundraising is ministry, there's no other word. And it's under the direction of the Spirit. Make certain you look through the right lens. It's a lens that sees through the heart, listens with the heart, and connects hearts with the heartbeat of the ministry.
Process	Lead with a process. Make certain there's a team in place that's responsible for the development work. Every board member should understand and agree on the assumptions underlying the development strategy that encourages total board participation in some way. Make certain there's an annual development plan in place, and check points to make certain you are on track. Understand the roles of all involved and how the plan will be evaluated, updated and ultimately achieved. Know how you will measure it. Not just in terms of resources raised, but things that are part of the development strategy...like number of visits to connect with donors or potential donors.

John Frank & Scott Rodin

"There may be no more important work a board does to support the development goals of the organization than to ensure that it remains a strong, involved, committed, and generous board."[139]

---

[138] Freeman, *Unlacing the Heart*, 66.
[139] Frank and Rodin, *Development 101*, 30.

Session 19 ◆ The Board's Role in Embracing the Donor (Part 2)

☑ ROLE NO. 2: ADVOCACY

Board members should be vocal supporters of the ministry and its development efforts. They should fully understand Biblical stewardship and advocate for stewards to invest in the ministry.

Critical Role of your Theology of Development: Have a commitment to an "abundance mentality," that God owns everything and there's enough to fund all that He wants done. Watch for the scarcity mentality where you see other organizations as competition. Drive the scarcity mentality out, we worship a God of absolute abundance. This abundance flows through us as faithful stewards. Our goal is to raise up faithful stewards, to see God's people develop hearts rich towards Him. We want our partners to experience the joy of a faithful steward as they are connected to the heartbeat of the ministry.
- Biblical stewardship understood and adopted by the board
- Biblical stewardship is the guide to everything you do.

Two-fold advocacy involved:
- First, board members should be public advocates in their communities and among their peers and networks.
- Second, this advocacy has the focused dimension of opening doors and making introductions that may be strategic to the ministry.

☑ ROLE NO. 3: INVOLVEMENT

The third role of the board is involvement:
- Personal board involvement is key to a successful development effort. We lead by example.
- Remember, not all board members are alike. Every board member is unique and will have different levels of generosity and ways to participate in the process.
- See suggested chart to obtain the board's annual commitment to their involvement in the development work for the coming year.[140] We suggest modifying the chart slightly to include a place for GIK and volunteerism which are huge in camping.

"God funds what HE wants done!"

Stories of Sheer Pure Grace
Nancy L. Nelson[141]

---

[140] Frank and Rodin, *Development 101*, 38. (Figure 3: "Annual Board of Director's Commitment Form")
[141] Nancy L. Nelson, *Stories of Sheer Pure Grace*, 116.

Session 19 ◆ The Board's Role in Embracing the Donor (Part 2)

❑ 3. REVIEW: FOUR KEYS AND FOUR CAUTIONS!

☑ FOUR KEYS TO SUCCESS IN WORKING WITH YOUR BOARD:

❑ 1. Clear Expectations, Written and Reviewed

- Be sure your board documents include clear language that lays out the expectations of all board members regarding personal giving and participation in the plans of the ministry.

- In addition to clear articulation, it is critical that you add three disciplines:
    - **First,** be sure these expectations are openly shared and discussed with all potential new board members before they decide to join the board.
    - **Second,** review these expectations frequently at board meetings to reinforce the work everyone has agreed to take on when they joined.
    - **Third,** be willing to hold board members accountable for lack of performance in this area. This is the toughest part of the job for a board chair, but it is his/her responsibility to talk to board members who do not follow through on their responsibilities as a board member.

❑ 2. Training, Equipping and Support

- It's not enough to tell board members they need to help with development, they must be trained, equipped and supported to help them do so.

- By training we mean working with each board member to help them develop the skills they need to fulfill their expectations. Training needs to match expectations, so no board member feels they are being held responsible for actions they are not trained to do.

- By equipping we mean they need the tools (like a case statement) to carry out this work. Board members should be trained in how and when to use these tools, and the development leadership should be listening for what board members need to be successful, and ready to develop new tools as necessary to meet that need.

- By support we mean that board members should be able to call or email a development staff person (or development committee chair person, or executive director if there is no paid person) and get the advice and guidance they need as they carry out their work. There should also be a regular development training session at board meetings so board members are always up to date on the best tools and processes to be successful. Support also goes the other way.

❑ 3. Opening Doors and Making Strategic Connections

- Board members tend to underestimate the breadth of their contact network and the value it may have for their organization. These networks contain potential partners that can become major supporters (what are termed #1's of the segmented donor lists.)

- It is not enough to announce at a board meeting, "We need you to be introducing us to key people of wealth and influence." An important component of this work with board members is meeting with them one-to-one and talking through their contact network. Start small—have each board member think of just one person in their network to connect the organization to and how they will go about connecting them.

- Whatever the strategy, every board member can be actively involved in making strategic new connections for the ministry if they have a plan and are supported in carrying it out.

❑ 4. Accountability and Celebration

- When board members have success in carrying out their development responsibilities, CELEBRATE…dive into that HOOPLA bucket!

- Nothing will motivate other board members more than the exciting reports of how fellow members are opening doors, building key relationships, and seeing God do amazing things through their faithfulness.

- Remember, board members are volunteers, and they need encouragement and celebration as much as any other volunteers.

☑ FOUR CAUTIONS IN WORKING WITH YOUR BOARD:

❏ 1. Make the Goals Realistic

- Be careful not to demotivate your board members by setting unrealistic goals for their work in development.

- Don't set specific dollar goals for board members to "raise," but set goals based on opening doors, making connections, and advocating for the ministry. If goals seem unreachable you have lost before you have even begun.

- Work with the board to discuss goals that reflect their skills, time commitments, and contact networks.

- Get buy-in and ownership of the goals from the outset and board members will partner with you to achieve them. This process needs to be driven within the board, not staff-driven.

❏ 2. Play to Each Member's Strengths

- Remember, not all board members are alike. Understand the unique strengths of each member and build a plan and set of goals that align with those strengths. If you haven't done it yet, have your board members take the CliftonStrengths® assessment.

- One major mistake made is designing a "one size fits all" approach to setting board goals. As you get to know each member, it will become clear how they are uniquely gifted and positioned to help your organization.

- Tailor a plan for them that fits that uniqueness and they will be more likely to achieve it.

❏ 3. Use Rewards Rather than Sticks

- Too often directors and development staff lament over the lack of board support and their remedy—sadly—is more accountability and a bigger stick.

- Most board members are passionate about the ministry and are demonstrating so by giving of their time to serve. The motivation is there, it usually just needs to be fanned like warm coals into an actual fire.

- Try more encouragement, more rewards, and the right training, equipping, and support— and you will see your board members step up to their responsibilities and enjoy doing so. *Think rewards, not sticks.*

❏ 4. Finally—Remember What Development Is Really All About

- Board members are on the same journey as everyone else—to becoming more faithful stewards. That includes their own giving, use of their time and talents, and full surrender to being Kingdom-focused people.

- How do your interactions help them on their journey to "unlace their hearts?"

- Pray that God will use you to help every board member to be a more faithful steward, and that your own heart would be unlaced, and in the right place, as your work with them towards their development goals.

NOTES:

Session 19 ◆ The Board's Role in Embracing the Donor (Part 2)

❑ 4. TABLE WORK: INDIVIDUAL AND GROUP QUESTIONS

#1. MY ANSWERS:

CIRCLE:	ANSWER ON YOUR OWN
Yes No	#1. All of our board members have a clear understanding of their roles and responsibilities in supporting our development work, including expectations for their personal giving to our organization.
Yes No	#2. All of our board members feel they have been equipped and supported to carry out their responsibilities successfully.
#3. Our biggest struggle in getting our board involved in fundraising is:	

#2. NEXT: SHARE YOUR ANSWERS TO THE ABOVE 3 QUESTIONS WITH YOUR TEAM

NOTES:

#3. CHOOSE ONE KEY THAT WILL BEST ADDRESS YOUR ONE BIGGEST PROBLEM:

ONE KEY:	
	Create 1-2 steps you will take to introduce this key to your board:

#4. CHOOSE ONE CAUTION THAT WILL BEST ADDRESS YOUR ONE BIGGEST PROBLEM:

ONE CAUTION:	
	How will you communicate the caution to your board and what accountability will you put in place to be sure you avoid this problem?

SESSION 20

Coach Time

☑ Our Strategic Next Steps
☑ Healthy Governance Checklist

SESSION 20:
Coach Time:
☑ Our Strategic Next Steps
☑ Healthy Governance Checklist

IN THIS SESSION (with your coach):

❑ 1. <u>Finalize</u>: Our Strategic Next Steps (see worksheets in Session 21)

❑ 2. <u>Prioritize</u>: Healthy Governance Checklist

Session 20 ◆ Coach Time: Our Strategic Next Steps and Healthy Governance Checklist

❏ 2. PRIORITIZE: HEALTHY GOVERNANCE CHECKLIST

☑ **HEALTHY GOVERNANCE CHECKLIST**
CCCA Thriving Boards ◆ Growing Healthy, Effective Boards

#1. EVERY BOARD MEMBER UNDERSTANDS THE THREE BOARD HATS.
- ❏ The GOVERNANCE hat is policy-oriented and worn only during board meetings (and never when volunteering).
- ❏ The VOLUNTEER hat is optional and is not worn during board meetings.
- ❏ The PARTICIPANT hat is worn at "required attendance" events for board members (identified a year in advance).
- ❏ *The Board Member Annual Affirmation Statement* details the roles and responsibilities of board members (based on the three hats) and this document is signed and affirmed by all board members every January.

See pages 10-12 for the complete "Healthy Governance Checklist."

Over the next 12 months, we will address the following segments of the Healthy Governance Checklist:

SESSION #	TOPIC	TARGET DATE

NOTES:

SESSION 21

Strategic Next Steps and My One Big Take-Away

SESSION 21:
Strategic Next Steps and My One Big Take-Away

IN THIS SESSION:

❏ 1. <u>Personal</u>: My One Big Take-Away

❏ 2. <u>With Your Coach</u>: Coaching Process Options

❏ 3. <u>Memo to Executive Director</u>: "Our Top-5 Strategic Next Steps"

Session 21 ◆ Strategic Next Steps and My One Big Take-Away

❑ 1. PERSONAL: MY ONE BIG TAKE-AWAY

My Name: _____

➔ Share Your Top Take-Away (at your table):

1	

213 | Thriving Boards Workbook ◆ 4th Edition

Session 21 ♦ Strategic Next Steps and My One Big Take-Away

❏ 2. WITH YOUR COACH: COACHING PROCESS OPTIONS
(more details will be presented in this session)

Our Coach is: _____

Two Days of Coaching Provided by CCCA With Flexible Options!
- ❏ One day on-site: _____, 20____
- ❏ One day for projects, phone coaching, etc.
  (or a second day on-site, later in the year, with travel covered by our camp)

- ❏ Two days on-site: _____, 20____

Review the following pages to discern where your coach may be of help to you:

BOARD ENRICHMENT/TRAINING

✓	COACH THE BOARD AND/OR CEO, OR COMMITTEE, ON YOUR MOST STRATEGIC NEXT STEPS:

Place an * by the three most strategic next steps.

❏ 3. Memo to Executive Director: "Our Top-5 Strategic Next Steps"

"OUR TOP-5 STRATEGIC NEXT STEPS"

MEMO

TO: **Executive Directors of Participating Camps**
CCCA THRIVING BOARDS

FROM: Ed McDowell
Project Coordinator

RE: Thriving Boards Program: Strategic Next Steps

Attached is a document, **"Our Top-5 Strategic Next Steps."** Based on the work you accomplished during the Fall Session, please complete the worksheet and HAND DELIVER IT. We will arrange to make a copy for both you and your coach.

Your list does not need to be perfect or absolutely your final/final "Top-5." But, hopefully, it will reflect the good work, discussion, interaction and discernment you engaged in together.

Please submit this during Session 21:

	3 OPTIONS	See flipchart in meeting room:
Option 1:	Hand Deliver	To:
Option 2:	Email the digital Word document	Email:
Option 3:	Email a photo of your list	Mobile:

Session 21 ◆ Strategic Next Steps and My One Big Take-Away

"OUR TOP-5 STRATEGIC NEXT STEPS"

3 OPTIONS→ Hand Deliver, Email the Digital Document, or Email Photo of Document

Camp/Conference Center	
Executive Director	
Name of person who completed this form:	
Today's date:	

As a result of our participation in the Spring Session of the CCCA THRIVING BOARDS program, here are our "Top-5 Strategic Next Steps" related to board leadership and development.

Top-5 Strategic Next Steps – Board Leadership and Development

POINT PERSON	STRATEGIC NEXT STEPS	NEED COACH'S HELP?	DEADLINE	DONE DATE
	1)	❑ Yes ❑ No		
	2)	❑ Yes ❑ No		
	3)	❑ Yes ❑ No		
	4)	❑ Yes ❑ No		
	5)	❑ Yes ❑ No		

APPENDIX

Recommended:
☑ Books
☑ Resources

APPENDIX:
Recommended Books and Resources

CONTENTS

No.	RESOURCE	PAGE
1	Best Board Books	219
2	Effective Board and Committee Meeting Tips	221
3	Resources for the Board's Role in Embracing the Donor	223
4	Two Worksheets Used by Murdock Trust to Assess Sustainability of Camps and Conference Centers	228
5	What Is Policy Governance	232
6	Organizations	235

APPENDIX ◆ Recommended Books and Resources

☐ 1. "BEST BOARD BOOKS"
ecfagovernance.blogspot.com

Brief reviews, by John Pearson, of 18 governance books featured on the ECFA blog, *Governance of Christ-Centered Organizations*:

http://ecfagovernance.blogspot.com/2019/03/best-board-books-index-to-18-good.html

☑ **PICK ONE:**

☐ Book #1: *Boards That Lead: When to Take Charge, When to Partner, and When to Stay Out of the Way*, by Ram Charan, Dennis Carey and Michael Useem

☐ Book #2: *The Imperfect Board Member: Discovering the Seven Disciplines of Governance Excellence*, by Jim Brown

☐ Book #3: *Best Practices for Effective Boards*, by E. LeBron Fairbanks, Dwight M. Gunter II, and James R. Cauchenour

☐ Book #4: *Stewards of a Sacred Trust: CEO Selection, Transition and Development for Boards of Christ-centered Organizations*, by David L. McKenna

☐ Book #5: *Owning Up: The 14 Questions Every Board Member Needs to Ask*, by Ram Charan

☐ Book #6: *Serving as a Board Member: Practical Guidance for Directors of Christian Ministries*, by John Pellowe

☐ Book #7: *The Nonprofit Board Answer Book: A Practical Guide for Board Members and Chief Executives (3rd Edition)*, published by BoardSource

☐ Book #8: *The Practitioner's Guide to Governance as Leadership: Building High-Performing Nonprofit Boards*, by Cathy A. Trower

☐ Book #9: *Called to Serve: Creating and Nurturing the Effective Volunteer Board*, by Max De Pree

Called to Serve, by Max De Pree

☑ Just 91 pages!
☑ Read the blog series by John Pearson and the index to 30 blogs:

http://ecfagovernance.blogspot.com/2017/10/called-to-serve-no-board-detail-is-too.html

☐ Book #10: *Good Governance for Nonprofits: Developing Principles and Policies for an Effective Board*, by Fredric L. Laughlin and Robert C. Andringa

APPENDIX ◆ Recommended Books and Resources

❑ Book #11: *Boards That Make a Difference: A New Design for Leadership in Nonprofit Organizations*, by John Carver

❑ Book #12: *Call of the Chair: Leading the Board of the Christ-centered Ministry*, by David L. McKenna

❑ Book #13: *Nonprofit Sustainability: Making Strategic Decisions for Financial Viability*, by Jeanne Bell, Jan Masaoka and Steve Zimmerman

❑ Book #14: *Scaling Up: How a Few Companies Make It…and Why the Rest Don't – Mastering the Rockefeller Habits 2.0*, by Verne Harnish

❑ Book #15: *Lessons From the Nonprofit Boardroom: 40 Insights for Better Board Meetings, (Second Edition)*, by Dan Busby and John Pearson

Lessons From the Nonprofit Boardroom
by Dan Busby and John Pearson

☑ 40 short lessons!
☑ Buy one for every board member!
☑ Bulk pricing at: www.ecfa.org/LessonsNonprofitBoardroom/
☑ Read the guest blogger series by leading CEOs and board members:

nonprofitboardroom.blogspot.com/

❑ Book #16: *The Council: A Biblical Perspective on Board Governance*, by Gary G. Hoag, Wesley K. Willmer, and Gregory J. Henson

❑ Book #17: *Lessons From the Church Boardroom: 40 Insights for Exceptional Governance*, by Dan Busby and John Pearson

Lessons From the Church Boardroom
by Dan Busby and John Pearson

☑ 40 short lessons!
☑ Buy one for every board member!
☑ Bulk pricing at: www.ecfa.church/LessonsChurchBoardroom/
☑ Read the guest blogs by leading pastors and church board members:

churchboardroom.blogspot.com/

❑ Book #18: *Humility*, by Andrew Murray

> "Humility is the only soil in which the graces root;
> the lack of humility is the sufficient explanation
> of every defect and failure."

APPENDIX ◆ Recommended Books and Resources

❏ 2. EFFECTIVE BOARD AND COMMITTEE MEETING TIPS

7 BASIC TIPS

PICK ONE THIS MONTH!	TOOL OR TEMPLATE
❏ **1.** Board and Committee Charter (or "job description")	☑ ECFA Knowledge Center: www.ECFA.org* ☑ BoardSource: www.BoardSource.org
❏ **2.** Chairperson	☑ Board Chair Job Description *ECFA Tools and Templates for Effective Board Governance*
❏ **3.** Annual S.M.A.R.T. Goals (3 to 5 for each committee)	☑ **Examples:** *ECFA Tools and Templates* Customize the "Monthly Dashboard Report" format for each committee report (monthly or quarterly). ❏ <u>Nominating Committee</u>: "Grow the board prospect pipeline to X candidates by Dec. 1, 2020." ❏ <u>Finance Committee</u>: "Update the BPM Executive Parameters section to ensure it addresses the sustainability goals in the Rolling 3-Year Strategic Plan." ❏ _____: ❏ _____:
❏ **4.** Clarify approval functions between the board, the CEO, senior staff, and the committee.	☑ Prime Responsibility Chart *ECFA Tools and Templates*
❏ **5.** Agenda	☑ Customize the board meeting agenda for use in your board meetings and committee meetings. *ECFA Tools and Templates*
❏ **6.** Minutes	☑ ECFA: "Recording Governing Board Minutes" http://www.ecfa.org/Content/Recording-Governing-Board-Minutes
❏ **7.** Reporting	☑ The "5/15" Monthly Report to the Board *ECFA Tools and Templates*

*ECFA Knowledge Center – A robust resource for ECFA-Accredited Members

Christian organizations and churches that meet the "Seven Standards of Responsible Stewardship™" qualify for ECFA Accreditation ("certification" for churches). To learn more, visit:

https://www.ecfa.org/Standards

MORE RESOURCES FOR COMMITTEES

☑ BOARD AND COMMITTEE MEETING MINUTES
"How much detail is too much (or too little)?"

"The minutes are not a transcript, nor should they try to be a verbatim account of the meeting. They simply should be a record of the decisions made and the action taken. When there is a debate or discussion to be recorded, only the major points for and against the issue at hand should be included. It is important for members to have meaningful discussions without being concerned about individual liability; therefore, names or direct quotations should not be recorded in relation to the debate."[142]

☑ Excerpt from Lesson 24 on Committee Nightmares!

SHOULD MOST STANDING COMMITTEES STAND DOWN?[143]
How many standing committees are needed for effective governance?

Read about the dysfunctional committee structure used by a ministry board. The committees were "fond of assigning research projects to staff. As a result, staff spent hundreds of hours each year studying issues that rarely ever result in committee action, let alone board action. This all falls under the heading of a standing committee nightmare."

5 QUESTIONS:
✓ How many standing committees should a board have?
✓ Which standing committees are most often used by boards?
✓ When should ad hoc committees and task forces be used?
✓ What can a board do when excessive standing committees are required by the ministry bylaws?
✓ How often should a board review its committee structure?

Dan Busby

"Ad hoc committees and task forces are one of the most under-used tools by boards. They are formed for a limited period of time to address a specific need."[144]

---

[142] "Board Meeting Minutes" posted by BoardSource at *https://boardsource.org/resources/board-meeting-minutes*.
[143] Dan Busby and John Pearson, *More Lessons From the Nonprofit Boardroom* (See Lesson 24).
[144] Ibid.

❑ 3. RESOURCES FOR THE BOARD'S ROLE IN EMBRACING THE DONOR

RESOURCES FROM:
ESSENTIALS OF DEVELOPMENT SEMINAR
M.J. MURDOCK CHARITABLE TRUST
Used by permission.[145]

ESSENTIALS of DEVELOPMENT

➔ **Note: The following pages are courtesy of the M.J. Murdock Charitable Trust's program, "Essentials of Development."**

The Essentials of Development Seminar is designed to help smaller or start-up organizations build a sustainable development structure. Over a pair of two-day sessions, a five-member faculty of Pacific Northwest leaders presents valuable materials and strategies to organizations.

DOWNLOAD SEMINAR MATERIALS:
https://murdocktrust.org/enrichment-programs/enrichment-program-trainings/essentials-development-seminar/

These past *Essentials of Development* seminar materials are in PDF format, except where noted:
- ❑ General Thoughts
- ❑ Priority Prospect List
- ❑ The Fundraising Case
- ❑ Major Gift Stewardship
- ❑ Annual Fund Development Plan
- ❑ Annual Fund Development Plan (Sample): PDF | Excel
- ❑ Annual Fund Development Plan (Template): PDF | Excel
- ❑ Development Team
- ❑ Strategic Planning
- ❑ SWOT Form: PDF | Word
- ❑ Strategic Plan Template: PDF | Word
- ❑ Taking Donors Seriously Manual

---

[145] © Copyright 2016. M.J. Murdock Charitable Trust. All Rights Reserved. www.MurdockTrust.org

RESOURCES FROM:
ESSENTIALS OF DEVELOPMENT SEMINAR – M.J. MURDOCK CHARITABLE TRUST
Used by permission.[146]

ESSENTIALS of DEVELOPMENT

THE FUND-RAISING CASE

BASIC CONSIDERATIONS

1) Fund-raising starts with commitment to a mission, not with awareness and understanding of financial need.

2) A well-designed Case will be valuable in staff recruitment, as a guide in planning programs, and as a central resource document for all fund-raising and public relations activities.

3) A Case is not intended simply to be given or sent to prospects but to be presented personally; consequently, the Case must be designed as a presentation tool for the staff and volunteer presenters and not simply as a brochure to be read by prospects.

4) Fund-raising without a Case is like running a business without a business plan.

[146] © Copyright 2016. M.J. Murdock Charitable Trust. All Rights Reserved. www.MurdockTrust.org

APPENDIX ◆ Recommended Books and Resources

RESOURCES FROM:
ESSENTIALS OF DEVELOPMENT SEMINAR – M.J. MURDOCK CHARITABLE TRUST
Used by permission.[147]

ESSENTIALS of DEVELOPMENT

THE FUND-RAISING CASE

COMPONENTS

1) THEME

What is the most succinct phrase to summarize your mission statement?

Start with a verb and bring out your "niche." Give donors and prospects a "handle" for knowing and remembering your bottom line.

2) NEED

If your prospects are not individuals served by your organizations, a statement of need at the outset of your Case is essential. Describe it graphically and lead up to why your organization is needed.

3) THE MISSION

Why is your organization in business?

Focus on fundamental reasons, on what you are. Focus on your unique qualities, separating your organization from "the pack."

4) DESIRED IMPACT

What are the long-term results you envision for the individuals you serve and the community they represent?

Describe your organization's long-term impact on individuals' lives, the character you're committed to developing—"the product" of your organization.

5) PROGRAM

What are the programs and activities your organization employs to carry out your mission to achieve your goals?

---

[147] © Copyright 2016. M.J. Murdock Charitable Trust. All Rights Reserved. www.MurdockTrust.org

6) ACCOMPLISHMENTS/IMPACT

What evidence is there that your program is achieving the goals you've set out?

Share stories of young people you serve, who have been impacted by your organization, and if appropriate, list objective data demonstrating your impact and accomplishments.

7) THE FUTURE

Where is your organization headed over the long-term?

Paint the vision in broad strokes and relate it back to your mission and goals. Make it exciting but don't exaggerate. Relate it to why you're raising money now, making it clear that by investing in the current development program your donors are leading the way to fulfilling this future vision.

8) DEVELOPMENT PLAN

What is the entity (e.g., campus, area, etc.), the overall goal? When do you need it? What do you need it for? How much do you need for each of the components?

9) GIFT PLANS

What is your strategy based on your donor list, and how many are already giving at what amounts? List the number of gifts needed at each level starting at the highest on down, including what you have and those you hope to have based on your strategy.

For gifts at levels above $100 per month, present in annual terms. At $100 and on down, present as monthly gifts.

10) PROFILE

What are the basic facts about your organization? Who are the people your organization serves? Who are the key players leading your organization and programs?

APPENDIX ◆ Recommended Books and Resources

RESOURCES FROM:
ESSENTIALS OF DEVELOPMENT SEMINAR – M.J. MURDOCK CHARITABLE TRUST
Used by permission.[148]

ESSENTIALS of DEVELOPMENT

DEVELOPING A CASE STATEMENT

TEN QUESTIONS TO ASK YOURSELF:

1) What one phrase captures your program?

2) Why is your organization needed?

3) What are the essential parts of your organization?

4) Look at the individuals you are serving; what difference do you make to them?

5) What are the programs or activities of your organization that make a difference?

6) What has your organization done to meet its goals?

7) In the next 3 years, where is your organization headed?

8) How much is the budget of your organization?

9) How can you break down your annual plan into areas?

10) Who are the key players in your organization?

[148] © Copyright 2016. M.J. Murdock Charitable Trust. All Rights Reserved. www.MurdockTrust.org

❏ 4. Two Worksheets Used by Murdock Trust to Assess Sustainability of Camps and Conference Centers

The following two worksheets will be referenced in:

Session 14: The Board's Financial/Fiduciary Role: Long-Term Sustainability

Would a foundation view your organization as floundering or flourishing?

Adapted from tools used by:
M.J. Murdock Charitable Trust[149]

---

[149] For more information on M.J. Murdock Charitable Trust, visit www.MurdockTrust.org.

CAMP REVENUE REVIEW AND PROJECTIONS

MARKETS	Prior Fiscal Year		Current Completed Fiscal Year		Three Years From Now Projections		
					Anticipated Revenue		
	# of Donors	$ Amount Received	# of Donors	$ Amount Received	# of Donors	Low $ Amount	High $ Amount
Individuals < $1,000							
Individuals > $1,000							
Board							
Foundations							
Business /Corporations							
Associations/Churches							
Government							
Special Event #1							
Special Event #2							
Special Event #3							
Camper Fees							
Rental Groups							
Camp Store							
Other							
Total Revenues		$		$		$	$
Total Expenses		$		$		$	$

APPENDIX ◆ Recommended Books and Resources

CAMP QUANTITATIVE HISTORY
Key Benchmarks, Income and Expense – For Years Ending Dec. 31

BENCHMARKS		2014	2015	2016	2017	2018	2019
STAFF							
	Full Time Equiv. Year-round						
	FTE of Part Time Year-round						
	FTE of Part Time Summer						
	# Volunteers						
CAMP PROFILE							
	# Beds - All season						
	# Beds - Summer						
	# Camps Offered						
	Unduplicated CAMP Attendance						
	# Group Rentals						
	Undulplicated Rental Attendance						

OPERATIONS

Income

	2014	2015	2016	2017	2018	2019
Camp Fees						
Rental Fees						
Store Sales						
Contributions						
Other Income						
TOTAL	$	$	$	$	$	$

Expenses

	2014	2015	2016	2017	2018	2019
Salaries and Benefits						
Food						
Program						
Administration						
Occupancy						
Maintenance						
Other						
TOTAL	$	$	$	$	$	$

Operating Surplus/Deficit $ $ $ $ $ $

CAPITAL

		2014	2015	2016	2017	2018	2019
	Beginning Bldg Fund Cash	0					
plus:	Building Fund Gifts Rec'd	0					
minus:	Capital Expenditures	0					
equals:	**Ending Bldg Fund Cash**	$	$	$	$	$	$

CONTRIBUTED INCOME

	2014	2015	2016	2017	2018	2019
For Operations						
Amount Given $	$	$	$	$	$	$
# Donors giving > $1,000/year						
For Building Improvements						
Amount Given $	$	$	$	$	$	$
# Donors giving > $1,000/year						
For Endowment	$	$	$	$	$	$
Total Contributed $	$	$	$	$	$	$

❑ 5. What Is Policy Governance

What Is Policy Governance[150]

Looking for a precise description of the 10 principles of the Policy Governance model? This official document that lays out what IS and IS NOT Policy Governance.

POLICY GOVERNANCE® SOURCE DOCUMENT

Why a Source Document?
A "source" is a point of origin. A source document is a "fundamental document or record on which subsequent writings, compositions, opinions, beliefs, or practices are based." (Websters)

Without a simply expressed clear point of source, interpretations, opinions, writings and implementations may intentionally or unintentionally diverge from the originating intent and ultimately be undifferentiated. The point of source ("authoritative source") is John Carver, the creator of Policy Governance, with Miriam Carver his fellow master teacher.

Without a simply expressed clear source document, Policy Governance is not reliably grounded and not transferable as a paradigm of governance. It is left vulnerable to interpretation, adaptation and impotence. This document has been produced by the International Policy Governance Association and approved by John and Miriam Carver as being true to source.

What Policy Governance is NOT!
1. Policy Governance is not a specific board structure. It does not dictate board size, specific officers, or require a CEO. While it gives rise to principles for committees, it does not prohibit committees nor require specific committees.

2. Policy Governance is not a set of individual "best practices" or tips for piecemeal improvement.

---

[150] Accessed on July 15, 2019.
https://www.policygovernanceassociation.org/resources/principles-of-policy-governance.html
Produced by International Policy Governance Association in consultation with John and Miriam Carver, 2005-2007-2011. Policy Governance® is a registered service mark of John Carver. Used with permission. Copying permitted if attributed to source. If referenced as source document, must reference entire document and, if copied, be copied in its entirety. August 2011

3. Policy Governance does not dictate what a board should do or say about group dynamics, methods of needs assessment, basic problem solving, fund raising, managing change.

4. Policy Governance does not limit human interaction or stifle collective or individual thinking.

What Policy Governance IS!
Policy Governance is a comprehensive set of integrated principles that, when consistently applied, allows governing boards to realize owner-accountable organizations. Starting with recognition of the fundamental reasons that boards exist and the nature of board authority, Policy Governance integrates a number of unique principles designed to enable accountable board leadership.

Principles of Policy Governance

1. Ownership: The board connects its authority and accountability to those who morally if not legally own the organization—if such a class exists beyond the board itself—seeing its task as servant-leader to and for that group. "Owners," as used in the Policy Governance model, are not all stakeholders, but only those who stand in a position corresponding to shareholders in an equity corporation. Therefore, staff and clients are not owners unless they independently qualify as such.

2. Governance Position: With the ownership above it and operational matters below it, a governing board forms a distinct link in the chain of command or moral authority. Its role is commander, not advisor. It exists to exercise that authority and properly empower others rather than to be management's consultant, ornament, or adversary. The board—not the staff—bears full and direct responsibility for the process and products of governance, just as it bears accountability for any authority and performance expectations delegated to others.

3. Board Holism: The board makes authoritative decisions directed toward management and toward itself, its individual members, and committees only as a total group. That is, the board's authority is a group authority rather than a summation of individual authorities.

4. Ends Policies: The board defines in writing the (a) the results, changes, or benefits that should come about for (b) specified recipients, beneficiaries, or other targeted groups, and (c) at what cost or relative priority for the various benefits or various beneficiaries. These are not all the possible benefits that may occur, but are those that form the purpose of the organization, the achievement of which constitutes organizational success. Policy documents containing solely these decisions are categorized as Ends in the terminology of the Policy Governance model but can be called by whatever name a board chooses, as long as the concept is strictly preserved.

5. Board Means Policies: The board defines in writing those behaviors, values, practices, disciplines, and conduct of the board itself and of the board's delegation and accountability relationship with its own subcomponents and with the executive part of the organization. Because these are non-ends decisions, they are called board means to distinguish them from ends and staff means. All board behaviours, decisions and documents must be consistent with these pronouncements. In the terminology of the Policy Governance model, documents containing solely these decisions are categorized as Governance Process and Board-Management Delegation but can be called by whatever name a board chooses, as long as the concept is strictly preserved.

6. Executive Limitations Policies: The board makes decisions with respect to its staff's means decisions and actions only in a proscriptive way in order simultaneously (a) to avoid prescribing means and (b) to put off limits those means that would be unacceptable even if theywork. Policy documents containing solely these decisions are categorized as Executive Limitations in the Policy Governance terminology, but can be called by whatever name a board chooses, as long as the concept is strictly preserved.

7. Policy "Sizes": The board's decisions in Ends, Governance Process, Board-Management Delegation, and Executive Limitations are made beginning at the broadest, most inclusive level and, if necessary, continuing into more detailed levels that narrow the interpretative range of higher levels, proceeding one articulated level at a time. These documents are exhaustive, replacing or obviating board expressions of mission, vision, philosophy, values, strategy, and budget. They are called policies in the terminology of the Policy Governance model but can be called by whatever name a board chooses, as long as the concept is strictly preserved.

8. Delegation to Management: If the board chooses to delegate to management through a chief executive officer, it honors the exclusive authority and accountability of that role as the sole connector between governance and management. In any event, the board never delegates the same authority or responsibility to more than one point.

9. Any Reasonable Interpretation: In delegating decisions beyond the ones recorded in board policies, the board grants the delegatee the right to use any reasonable interpretation of those policies. In the case of Ends and Executive Limitations when a CEO exists, that delegate is the CEO. In the case of Governance Process and Board-Management Delegation, that delegatee is the CGO (chief governance officer) except when the board has explicitly designated another board member or board committee.

10. Monitoring: The board monitors organizational performance solely through fair but systematic assessment of whether a reasonable interpretation of its Ends policies is being achieved within the boundaries set by a reasonable interpretation of its Executive Limitations policies. If there is a CEO, this constitutes the CEO's evaluation.

All other practices, documents, and disciplines must be consistent with the above principles. For example, if an outside authority demands board actions inconsistent with Policy Governance, the board should use a 'required approvals agenda' or other device to be lawful without compromising governance.

Policy Governance is a precision system that promises excellence in governance only if used with precision. These governance principles form a seamless paradigm or model. As with a clock, removing one wheel may not spoil its looks but will seriously damage its ability to tell time. So in Policy Governance, all the above pieces must be in place for Policy Governance to be effective. When all brought into play, they allow for a governing board to realize owner accountability. When they are not used completely, true owner accountability is not available.

Policy Governance boards live these principles in everything they are, do and say.

APPENDIX ◆ Recommended Books and Resources

❑ 6. Organizations

Find more board governance resources at:

❑ **CHRISTIAN CAMP AND CONFERENCE ASSOCIATION**
www.CCCA.org
- National Conventions, Sectional Meetings, Webinars
- *InSite Magazine* ("On Board" column)

❑ **ECFA** (Evangelical Council for Financial Accountability)
www.ECFA.org
- Blog: "Governance of Christ-Centered Organizations"
  http://ecfagovernance.blogspot.com/
- Webinars, Governance Knowledge Center, newsletters
- ECFA Governance Toolbox Series
- Accreditation

❑ **BOARDSOURCE**
www.BoardSource.org
- Publications, resources, surveys

www.ingramcontent.com/pod-product-compliance
Lightning Source LLC
Chambersburg PA
CBHW081425220526
45466CB00008B/2277